WHAT PEOI
Will the Real C

Satan would love nothing more tha.. ... ..ure God's people from the truth of Jesus Christ and eternal salvation right within the walls of the visible church. John writes, "Beloved, do not believe every spirit, but test the spirits to see whether they are from God, for many false prophets have gone out into the world" (1 John 4:1). Dr. Richard does a masterful job of revealing the spirits in many false churches in a delightful, readable style, while always keeping the eyes of the reader fixed on Jesus, the author and perfecter of our faith.

Rev. Dr. James Baneck, executive director, LCMS Pastoral Education

....

Rev. Dr. Matthew Richard has done it again! He carefully paints a realistic picture of the twenty-first-century American church, where a "church shopping" family hears messages focused on things like the beauty of the buildings, social connections, serving the community, and self-improvement. What makes the Christian Church different? Christ and Him crucified. Matthew Richard candidly, yet with a pastoral heart, points us to our only hope: Christ's gifts of forgiveness, life, and salvation. What a joy to know we have a faithful resource for all the baptized to discern how to find a faithful Christian congregation.

Rev. Brady Finnern, president, LCMS Minnesota North District

....

Popular estimation would have us believe that congregations are more or less interchangeable. However, even a casual observer can see the many distinctions between Christian congregations. Which differences matter? Which do not? And above all, what should unite a church and what should it be oriented toward? Pastor Richard's thorough and easy-to-read analysis helps the reader navigate the complex reality of the contemporary church scene by showing how Christ is the foundation and goal of all things in our lives together in Christian congregations.

Rev. Christopher Brademeyer, pastor, St. John's Lutheran Church, Oakes, North Dakota

....

....

"What should I look for in a church?" Today, pluralism has rendered this practical and pressing question hopelessly complicated by ever-multiplying answers and options. Or is it so complicated? Matthew Richard gets to the bottom of things without compromising the depth of insight or fidelity to the Scriptures. His latest book is an accessible read for anyone looking for a new church home or for any Christian who wants to identify the criteria that make for the true church.

Caleb Hoverson, seminarian, Concordia Theological Seminary, Fort Wayne, Indiana

....

With piercing insight, Rev. Dr. Matthew Richard presents seven archetypal pseudo-churches that are unified and built around things other than Christ. While operating as a trustworthy, practical guide as to which types of churches to avoid, this book also sounds a clarion warning to true churches of what to guard against so as not to have their lampstands removed. Although you may find some of these false churches painfully familiar, hopefully you have finally found a home in the true church.

Andrew Allis, BA, philosophy and theology, Boston College; MDiv, Assemblies of God Theological Seminary, Springfield, Missouri; ThM, Presbyterian Church in America, Covenant Theological Seminary, Creve Coeur, Missouri

....

This book is an eye-opening look at why churches can seem so different in form and function. Why are some churches so formal while others have coffee shops right in the building? Why do some encourage children to be separate from the adults? Why do some have praise bands and some have organs? Why do some celebrate the Lord's Supper every week and some twice a year? Why do some encourage outreach and mission work while others focus on their own small groups and church activities? In this book, Pastor Richard helps the reader understand that not any one of these things makes a real church. Rather, a real church's primary focus is gathering its congregation around Christ's Word and Sacrament.

Erin Hagemeister, parishioner, St. Paul's Lutheran Church, Minot, North Dakota

....

WILL THE

Real Church

please stand up?

• • • • • • • • • • •

7 FALSE CHURCHES

Matthew Richard

CONCORDIA PUBLISHING HOUSE • SAINT LOUIS

Published by Concordia Publishing House
3558 S. Jefferson Ave., St. Louis, MO 63118-3968
1-800-325-3040 • cph.org

1 2 3 4 5 6 7 8 9 10   33 32 31 30 29 28 27 26 25 24

To the baptized saints of
ST. PAUL'S LUTHERAN CHURCH OF MINOT, ND
1 CORINTHIANS 2:2

Contents

Acknowledgments

I want to express great gratitude to the following people for their assistance in writing this book.

First, Serenity, Matthias, Anya, and Alaythia, thank you for being joy in my life. Thank you for supporting me in this writing endeavor.

Second, thank you to Tina, Kimberly, Sharon, Erin, Jennifer, Nathan, Emilie, Joshua, Betty, Lauri, Leon, Carol, and Joanna. It is a privilege to be your pastor and friend; it is an honor to have had your help critiquing this book.

Third, thank you to my editor, Jamie. Your professionalism and editorial understanding have been most beneficial to this project.

Last, thank you to Concordia Publishing House for your encouragement and writing support. Thank you for being the church's publishing arm; thank you for the opportunity to write for God's baptized saints.

Sub Cruce

Preface

We like to establish gathering points. Cozy campfires, coffee tables, movie rooms, sports fields, and dinner tables attract our attention and invite us to belong. There is nothing wrong with gathering around a campfire, coffee table, television, or any other object. It is good to roast marshmallows with the family around the fire. Gathering around a football field and cheering for a team is good. Sipping coffee and talking with friends around a table is good. This is all good. However, is it possible that all this gathering goodness can be harmful? When we gather around objects, ideas, or things we fear, love, and trust (rather than around the Lord, who calls us to fear, love, and trust in Him), we can suddenly find ourselves in a gathering where Christ is not present at all. This is what happens when churches substitute the foundation of the church with something else entirely—something that seems good, a gathering that feels good, an environment that invites us to belong to something other than Christ. (See 1 Corinthians 3:10–13.)

There was a remarkable gathering in the Old Testament book of Genesis. We read of an ancient group who united to build an impressive city with a tower reaching the sky. Their sights were set on the heavens, and they had the unity to accomplish their lofty goal. However, the people did not build the tower for God or for His church; God did not need a tower. They built this original skyscraper for their own glory. Indeed, the people attached their names to the tower to commemorate *their* greatness. Together as one, they climbed higher and drew closer to heaven by their own strength and ingenuity. Their great endeavor became a rallying point for mankind—a monument to humanity's elaborate schemes to advance the human race and live with complete independence. Many scholars believe that the people built the tower to ensure salvation from any potential floods. This man-made tower was a central unifying point for mankind's greatness, built with the seemingly noble purpose of saving humanity from any future catastrophic acts of God. (See Genesis 11:1–9.)

The tower of Babel never reached its pinnacle. Yet the fervor to work toward heaven remains, as mankind continues to gather around self-erected towers in an attempt to get closer to heaven and experience unity. As we scan the horizon of Christendom, we can see present-day towers of Babel. Objects and ideas are lifted to heights of glory where people gather in today's churches and worship. Tragically, even though many churches bear the name of Christ, they unite around lofty Christless towers, striving for what they deem is the church's end goal. In the end, these towers draw them up and away from the name of Christ, making them false churches.

My first book, *Will the Real Jesus Please Stand Up?*, focused on the twelve false christs in today's churches. Now I invite you to this sequel, which scans the horizon of Christendom in the twenty-first century to focus on seven tall towers—seven false churches—that, like Babel, will crumble and fall. By the end of this book, we will see which church is left standing, in essence asking, *"Will the Real Church Please Stand Up?"*

Meet the Campbells

"Jessica, which box is the remote in?" Ben yelled.

"I think it was tossed into one of those apple boxes in the bedroom," Jessica yelled back from the kitchen.

Ben made his way through the maze of boxes in the living room and pushed open the bedroom door. The boxes were stacked three to four feet high, and since the majority were old apple boxes from a local grocery store, the room had a sweet but musty smell. Ben sighed as he stared blankly at the boxes before mumbling to himself, "A needle in a haystack. There are, like, twenty apple boxes."

As frustration built in Ben, Jessica came in and put her arm around him, smiling with love. "Ah, cheer up, you old scrooge. It's right over here." Jessica walked past Ben and grabbed an apple box labeled "Misc." She opened it up, and right there at the top was the lost remote.

Handing it over, she chirped, "Here you go, Mr. Scrooge. Now you can watch the baseball game while you unpack the rest of the boxes in the living room."

Ben smiled, not because Jessica found the remote, but because he felt her love in the sarcastic jab.

As Jessica reached over to close the apple box, she noticed the side of a book from their previous church. An elderly lady had given it to them when they were married at Redeemer Church fifteen years ago, back in Fairview. She grabbed the book, held it up, and motioned to her husband. "Hey, Ben, we need to find a church!"

Ben, looking at the book, recalled that it was dear Betsy who had given them the book. She had wrapped it in a unique greenish paper, and it had a strong scent of old ladies' perfume.

"Yeah, I guess it has been about six months. We kind of stopped going as we geared up for this move, didn't we? We should get back into a church, especially now that we don't have close family around us," Ben said with a touch of guilt coloring his voice.

Nodding her head with the same guilty conviction displayed on her face, Jessica replied, "Well, what's stopping us? Let's add it to our list of things to do. We found this perfect house, yesterday's meeting for Noah's soccer team went great, Olivia is excited about starting dance classes with the teacher who lives across the street, and I found that cute boutique on Thirty-Second Avenue, so let's find a church!"

Smiling, Ben responded, "Sounds good. Now if only I could find a perfect golf course that is forgiving to my nasty slice!"

• • • • • • • • • • • • • • • • • • • •

Meet the Campbells: Ben, Jessica, Noah, and Olivia. They recently moved to Midway, a growing city of approximately 250,000. Both Ben and Jessica are in their early forties, while Noah is just starting seventh grade and Olivia is beginning fourth. The Campbells are a typical middle-class family. Ben transferred to a new accounting firm in Midway, and Jessica was hired as a dental hygienist only five blocks from their new house. Six months before moving to Midway, though, the Campbells' church attendance had become sparse due to the busyness of the upcoming move. Furthermore, they had taken their previous church for granted, as it was their family church. Ben's dad was a longtime member of the church council, and Jessica's mom was very involved in a women's card-making group. In other words, since Ben, Jessica, Noah, and Olivia always had a church to call home, and since it was the only church they had ever known, they were unfamiliar with the differences in other churches and unsure of what key features to look for in a new church.

As the reader, you are invited to follow the Campbells as they experience the blessings and struggles of visiting eight very different churches in Midway. Think of yourself as a fly on the wall as they discover what exactly makes a "good church" in their journey to find a new church home. To help you as you journey with the Campbells, you will be given insights into interactions and observances. Each chapter will include various text boxes to provide an explanation of the concepts, features, and interactions that the Campbells encounter in their eight church visits. A study guide is included at the end of each chapter, with a leader guide at the end of the book. The text boxes, study guides, and leader guide will aid individual reflection or group conversation and help you gain an in-depth understanding of each chapter. In other words, as the reader, you will have a unique opportunity to observe the Campbells' reactions—why they are responding the way they are—and discern what is taking place at each church they visit.

With each church, the Campbells will be subconsciously wrestling with two simple yet important questions. Though they will not always be aware that they are trying to answer these questions, they will nonetheless be observing what continually **unites** the church and discussing what the **purpose** of each church is.

To make sure these two questions are clear for you, the reader, let's examine them a little more thoroughly.

Unity: What idea, action, or thing causes everyone to be united in harmony? What is at the center? What gives church members joy, satisfaction, assurance, or meaning? What keeps them coming back?

Purpose: What is the fundamental purpose or end of the church? Where is the message leading? Where does the church invest, devote, or commit all of its energy and focus? Where are the members of the church being led?

As previously stated, while these questions are fairly simple, they are also important. Furthermore, as you will discover with the Campbells, the unity and purpose of each church are clearly seen in the words, actions, architecture, and demeanor of each church they visit, even if not explicitly defined in official literature or posted on the churches' websites.

DOCTRINE AND PRACTICE

The architecture, practices, liturgy, programs, actions, and slogans of the church provide a framework for parishioners to live the life of faith. Some people believe that the methods of the church do not matter, that such frameworks are neutral. Thus, churches could theoretically use any framework or method because they are impartial and don't affect the church's theology. In other words, those people believe that doctrine and practice are separate.

However, doctrine and practice are more closely related than we often realize. In fact, doctrine is embedded in practice. If a church incorporates practices that work against their beliefs, over time, their doctrine will subtly change to accommodate the changed practices. That is to say, incorrect practices can bleed false theology into the church's core teaching. Conversely, if a church exchanges bad doctrine for good doctrine, their practices will inevitably change to reflect the good doctrine.

Thus, one can often learn the core doctrines of a given church by observing their architecture, practices, liturgy, programs, actions, and marketing slogans.

Now that we know a bit about the Campbells and we are focused on the important questions of unity and purpose, let's journey with the Campbells as they visit eight different churches in their new city and learn along with them what exactly makes a church real or false. Join the Campbells as they look for the real church to please stand up!

The Quest

"Hurry up, Olivia, we're going to be late!" yelled Ben. "Your mom and brother are already in the car."

"I'm coming, Dad!" Olivia yelled back, bounding down the stairs while putting on a light jacket.

Three minutes later, the Campbells were pulling out of their driveway in their gray SUV to travel to a church named The Quest.

After a twenty-minute drive to the eastern part of Midway, near the city mall, they approached what used to be a large retail store. The building had obviously been remodeled, and a large, bright, trendy sign displaying "THE QUEST" invited the family to start their spiritual adventure. Ben turned into the parking lot—an extremely full parking lot.

Jessica gasped. "Are we late?"

Looking back and forth for an open spot, Ben responded, "I don't think so. Their website listed ten thirty as one of the service times. We've got at least fifteen minutes."

Almost interrupting, Jessica said with a bit of anticipation, "Oh, people are coming out now. They must be getting done with the first service."

The Campbells slowly maneuvered around a smiling couple holding coffee cups in their hands and circled the lot. Ben and

Jessica noticed a familiar decal on the back of many vehicles. It was the same church logo they had seen all over social media since moving to Midway: line-art binoculars with a cross in the center of the lenses. Just beneath the modern-looking logo, in the same edgy font from the front sign, was "THE QUEST."

THE CATCH-22 OF CHURCH MARKETING

Many churches will hire church marketers to conduct a demographic study. Churches then receive information about the people who live around the church: their ethnicity, age, education, habits, likes, and interests. This information can be helpful—a church surrounded by retirees likely wouldn't start a preschool, for example. But often, church leadership will narrow in on a particular group of people whom they want to attract to the sanctuary on Sundays, people to market to. (More often than not, it is "young people.") To attract whatever group they have homed in on, the church will adjust its architecture, music, language, attire, and branding to woo these people through the doors.

And there's the catch-22. Whatever a congregation uses to entice the people through their doors will be the same way the church will need to keep people inside the doors. For example, if a congregation uses a raffle for a flat-screen TV to attract people to come to church, they may get people through the doors. However, to keep those people inside, they will have to raffle a sound system as well. (See John 6:26.)

As Ben drove by the main entrance, he noticed a sign with an arrow that said "First-Time Parking."

Jessica, noticing the sign too, cheered, "Look, we get our very own parking space right in front!"

Before the Campbells could take off their seat belts, Noah looked out the window and said hesitantly, "Dad, who's that?"

A young woman with a blue shirt, sunglasses, and a beaming smile was walking toward the Campbells' SUV.

"I'm not sure, bud," Ben replied.

As soon as Ben stepped out of the SUV, a kind voice welcomed, "Hi there! Welcome to The Quest. My name is Abby. It's your first time here, right?"

Ben and Jessica both nodded their heads as they closed the car doors.

"Great. Let me show you around!" Abby said energetically, leading them toward the entrance.

As they walked, Abby asked, "So how did you come to hear about The Quest?"

Ben responded, "I was online the other day and saw an advertisement that said, 'Looking for a new church home? Join The Quest!' And so I tapped it to learn more."

Nodding her head, Abby replied, "It's amazing how many people in Midway are not satisfied with their church. We hear from new members all the time that they are so glad they switched over to The Quest from their previous church."

Abby led them past some large windows that had the church logo and floor-to-ceiling posters of people adventuring through life. One of the windows featured a movie poster for *Deception Friday*, the latest blockbuster; however, it was modified to include "Sermon Series: May 21–June 25."

Noah noticed the poster right away. "Cool, Dad, check that out. It's the movie I was just telling you about."

The aroma of freshly brewed coffee grew stronger as they entered the church, and there was a feeling of high energy and anticipation—like the vibe and noise in a concessions area before a basketball game. Abby happily chatted with the Campbells as they made their way through the crowded lobby. Just before a coffee area, Abby motioned to a hallway, saying, "Let's go check in your kids with Miss Tina. She is in charge of the Kids' Quest and the Youth Quest."

Jessica nodded, indicating that she had heard Abby, but she was a bit confused. She leaned forward to project her voice through the noise. "What do you mean, 'check in'?"

Abby responded, "Oh, sorry. Yes, both of your kids will go to our Kids' and Youth Quest programs. Miss Tina will set up an app on your phone so that you can be contacted during the service if any issues arise. The kids will love it, as they can get church on their level, and you and your husband will be able to enjoy the service together. It is a fun and engaging environment."

DIVIDED-FAMILY VERSUS FAMILY-INTEGRATED CHURCHES

Separating children from the rest of the congregation during worship is a relatively new occurrence, originating in the nineteenth and twentieth centuries. While there is much history around this issue that can and should be debated, perhaps a more important question looms: Why? Are children removed so that they can be catechized and taught the Christian faith at a level suitable to their educational capacity, or are they removed as a means of childcare to allow adults to enjoy a professional church service without the interruptions of noisy children? And beyond the "why" of children's church, we should also ask whether it's necessary at all. That is, should the family be divided at the door of the church? Even though some churches have good intentions, the family is the core unit created by God. The world spends much time during the week dividing the family on the basis of systematic age segregation. However, do actions like this strengthen or weaken the family? (See Malachi 4:4–6; Psalm 78:5–8.)

After Ben and Jessica downloaded the app on their phones and Olivia and Noah were situated, Abby led them back to the main entrance, where they were able to order freshly brewed coffee. The coffee was made by several enthusiastic church volunteers and came in cups with The Quest logo. Coffees in hand, Ben and Jessica were guided into the auditorium, where they sat down in padded blue theater-like seats. Abby smiled and gave them a quick wave before leaving to attend to other duties. Ben placed his coffee cup in the spot on the armrest, noticing a red button. He pressed it, and his chair moved back several inches.

"Whoa, Jess, check this out," Ben marveled.

Meanwhile, Jessica was noticing the ceiling. The air duct system, pipes, and wires were all showing, yet they were painted black. The jet-black paint added depth and gave the auditorium a utilitarian design that reminded her of an episode of her favorite home-and-garden television show.

Then the overhead lights dimmed. Ben and Jessica's eyes were drawn toward two very large screens at the front of the auditorium, one placed on each side of a stage. The screens displayed bright, commercial-like videos. The first commercials promoted a small-group gathering going on in the church as well as information about an upcoming sermon series. A slide flashed on the screens, saying, "Do I need to dress up for church?" As the question faded, the next slide stated, "No. The Quest is a casual and friendly environment, so there is no dress code. Come in whatever is comfortable for you!"

A third commercial really grabbed Ben and Jessica's attention. The video highlighted something called "Journey Steps." From what Ben and Jessica gathered, the Journey Steps were ways in which attendees could further their spiritual quest. The first Journey Step was simply attending Sunday gatherings at The Quest. The video explained, "We are excited that you took the first step to show up and be here as the kingdom of God continues to expand in Midway."

The second step was to sign up to be a member. Membership apparently consisted of meeting with one of the leaders of the church in a new members' class. The third step was to join a Journey Group, which seemed to be organized around particular age groups. The music intensified as the fourth step appeared. The fourth step was to join a "ministry" in the church—serving on the welcome committee, helping in the Kids' Quest, joining the music team, making Sunday coffee, and so on. As the video explained this fourth Journey Step, a picture of Abby flashed briefly.

Ben leaned over and whispered to Jessica, "Abby must be on step four."

Several seconds later, the music on the video intensified even more as the final Journey Step was displayed: leadership. This last segment showed leaders, staff members, and volunteers sitting in meetings, pointing at charts, and praying.

WHAT IS THE MINISTRY?

In the book of Acts, the apostles appointed seven men to manage the distribution of food so that they could devote themselves to "prayer and to the ministry of the word" (Acts 6:4). In other words, the proper understanding of the word *ministry* is tied to preaching the Word and administering the Sacraments. And so, if a particular action of a church is not dealing with Word and Sacrament, it cannot properly be called a *ministry*. That does not mean that it is bad or not needed, though. Instead, it could be classified as something else, such as mercy care, administration, and so on. (See also Acts 20:24; Romans 15:19.)

. . . .

Let's take a step back and examine everything the Campbell family has encountered so far. The sights, smells, and conversations all communicate specific messages and are intended to create specific responses. First, as mentioned in the introduction, let us reflect on the purpose of The Quest. What is the purpose, the end goal, of The Quest based on what the Campbells have witnessed?

This question is answered by the commercial for their "Journey Steps." The numbered steps and the crescendo of the music subtly emphasized step 5 as the pinnacle of the journey. And so, while it felt good for the Campbells to accomplish step 1 by simply showing up, they felt the nudge to move beyond mere church attendance to membership. However, since each step was part of a larger journey, the Campbells also felt the nudge that they would need to join a small group (step 3), be plugged into a ministry (step 4), and finally arrive at leadership (step 5). Consider the steps a bit more closely, though, and an obvious division is present. Steps 1–3 were aimed at bringing the Campbells into the life of the church; steps 4–5 were aimed at the Campbells being a part of a ministry and leadership for the sake of bringing other people into the life of the church.

And so, everyone in The Quest was either in the process of joining the church (steps 1–3) or attempting to get other people to join the church (steps 4–5). In a way, the steps were circular, which means that the members of the church were not really on a quest to reach a destination. Everyone was either joining or getting other people to join. Rather than a journey that eventually culminated at a destination, the final goal of The Quest was to get people to come along on the adventure. Alas, everyone was on a perpetual journey—always searching, never finding, always traveling, never arriving.

TELOS

In philosophy, the word *telos* refers to the fulfillment of a goal. It is a word that looks to the end purpose of something. Applying the word *telos* to a local church, we could ask, "What is the ultimate goal or purpose of the local church?" In other words, where are the members of a local church being led? (See 1 Corinthians 15:3-4.)

• • • • • • • • • • • • • • • • • • • •

Back to the Campbells' experience at The Quest. After the Journey Steps video ended, the side lights faded out, while the lights on the middle of the stage intensified. Ben looked at his watch and realized that they had been watching videos for about ten minutes. Six people entered from the sides of the stage and took their spots in front of instruments and microphones.

The person at the front of the stage looked up and whooped, "Hey, The Quest, what's up!"

To Ben and Jessica's surprise, everyone began to cheer as if at a concert. The cheering turned to a steady clapping as the screens flashed with what appeared to be the name of a song: "Alive in You." The song was extremely catchy with its chord progressions; the lyrics seemed familiar and repeated often enough to where Jessica was able to hum along. Ben appreciated the guitar riffs, admired the drum solo, and noticed that the lyrics seemed to serve the tune. The music was professional, catchy, moving, and inspiring. He couldn't really sing along, but a lot of the people around them were mostly clapping, humming, and swaying to the beat rather than singing, so he didn't feel like he stuck out.

WHO IS THE AUDIENCE IN CHRISTIAN WORSHIP?

In many church worship services, it is taught that we are the speakers—that we are the ones talking to God, calling on Him with praise. This perspective sees God as the audience of our worship. This is similar to pagan worship, where worshipers would come to their gods with offerings and requests to please the gods and hopefully get a favorable response to their requests. (See 1 Kings 18:26–29.)

Christian worship is completely different. God is the speaker, and we are the audience. He has called and invited us to be with Him, creating a chance for us to talk together. In both the Old and New Testaments, God's Word is the main focus of worship. Indeed, God talks, and we listen and respond. Through His Word, the Bible, God shows us who He is and what He does. He reveals our sin through His words of Law and then delivers salvation through His words of Gospel. (See Exodus 29:42–46.)

The center lights faded after fifteen minutes of songs, and another video projected on the screens. The video was extremely well edited, with engaging clips from a recent movie called *Deception Friday*. When the video ended, Ben and Jessica saw that the band had exited the stage, and another man dressed in casual pants with a black shirt walked to center stage, carrying a stool. A couple of smaller spotlights followed his movement. He said in a more subdued and serious voice, "Good morning, The Quest. Let's pray." After a thirty-second prayer, it was obvious that the man on the stage was the church's senior pastor.

"By now, I'm sure you all have seen the new movie *Deception Friday*. It's a family favorite at our house. My wife, Chelsea, brought Malachi and Zeke to the theater another two times this week." After a short pause, he sat down on the stool and continued,

"Today, we are going to continue our series of comparing biblical truth to the themes of this popular movie."

Due to the recent move to Midway, neither Ben nor Jessica had had a chance to see the movie everyone was talking about. With a bit of disappointment on her face, Jessica leaned over and whispered to Ben, "I hope he doesn't give away any spoilers."

Just then, Jessica's phone vibrated. It was a message from The Quest app. The message bubble said, "Hi mom." She clicked on the icon, and it was a picture of Olivia waving, wearing a cutout hat that said "Kids' Quest." Jessica smiled and put her phone back into her purse; then she refocused her attention on the front.

The pastor described the various characters of the movie and then made applications back to biblical characters. He was a very good speaker with great eye contact. He did not rush, and he allowed for long pauses to let his points settle in. Jessica looked over at Ben and noticed him chuckle at a joke the pastor had just made. This pastor was relatable and trendy, and he seemed so confident and passionate about what he was saying. He shared several personal stories, including one about a tattoo he got to honor his brother.

INTO THE BIBLE OR OUT OF THE BIBLE?

There are two ways in which the Bible is handled in the church. The first is called *eisegesis.* (from Greek, pronounced *eye-suh-JEE-sis*). *Eisegesis* means to read into the Bible. For example, the Word is typically interpreted through the culture, time, and context of a particular people. (See Jeremiah 23:16.) The second is called *exegesis*. *Exegesis* means to read out of the Bible; thus, the Word will interpret the culture, time, and context of a particular people. (See also 2 Timothy 4:1–5.)

Even though the sermon was nearly thirty minutes long, it seemed to pass by rather quickly. Jessica was glad the pastor hadn't shared the ending of *Deception Friday*, but she wished she had watched it before coming so she could have understood the characters better.

The praise band entered again while the pastor was finishing up, and the lead guitarist began to play a quiet melody on his guitar. The music of the guitar seemed to wrap around the words of the pastor until the music crescendoed with the pastor's final amen. As the pastor walked off the stage, his spotlight faded, and the lights increased as the praise band leader started to sing a song, chanting, "Lift your voice and sing, stand and praise the King," over and over. Everyone in the auditorium stood up, and the volume increased, as did the stage lights.

For the next ten minutes, one song led directly into the next as the praise band led the church in song with contagious energy. The sounds swelled and crashed about like waves. The fervor increased as the last song ended in a chorus about the Christian's quest to be loving and how the journey of love never ends. Ben looked at his watch again, and it was already 11:32. Time had really flown. The worship leader beamed and finished the song by saying, "We are so glad you are here at The Quest." Ben and Jessica could not help but feel energized.

DOES MUSIC COVER OR CLOTHE THE WORD?

The purpose of music in worship is to clothe the Word—to elevate it with beauty. Tragically, though, many of the lyrics in modern praise songs are intended to serve the music instead, as at The Quest. Instead of clothing God's Word, the music can unfortunately cover God's Word. (See Psalm 69:30.)

The song ended, and the auditorium lights came up, highlighting again the energy and noise they had experienced upon first entering the building. As they made their way through the crowd, Jessica spoke loudly to Ben, "I will go get the kids and meet you at the coffee station."

Ben made his way through the crowd to the coffee station. As he waited, a couple approached him. "Hi there. You must be new here," the man said.

Ben smiled and exchanged a bit of small talk with them, indicating that he and Jessica had just moved to Midway.

"We just love it here at The Quest. And," the man added, pointing to the coffee station with a smile, "the coffee is great. The music is powerful. The kids get to do their own thing. And Pastor Nick's sermons are so easy to listen to. I am so glad we were handed a flyer at that Christian concert we attended two years ago. One look at their website, and we had to check out The Quest in person. We've been here ever since."

Ben thanked the couple for introducing themselves, and they exchanged a bit more small talk. Just as they left, Ben turned and saw Olivia running toward him.

"Daddy, it was so awesome! Miss Tina helped me make this hat. She said if I come back next week, I can get a matching bracelet."

GROWING CHURCHES ON THE FRONT PAGE

Churches with growing numbers, additions to their buildings, and large mission projects are often spotlighted in denominational publications and city conversations as a great success. While there may be much to appreciate about these stories, what does it say about our ideas of "success" when we don't also highlight small churches that persist even in dying communities? Consider how profound it is that in a dying community, a church remains open even though the local grocery

store, post office, bar, and elementary school have closed.
Perhaps we should reconsider our markers of success. (See
1 Samuel 16:7.)

• • • • • • • • • • • • • • • • • • •

Let's step back again and ask the question about unity: What
idea, action, or thing united everyone at The Quest? What gave
church members joy, satisfaction, assurance, or meaning? What
kept them coming back? Again, consider everything that the
Campbells experienced at The Quest: the signage was easy to
spot, they had first-time parking, a personal representative was
there to assist them, fresh coffee was brewed, they had a small
break from the kids, Olivia got to make crafts, the app was easy
to use, their seating was padded, the videos were appealing, the
service was easy to follow, the lighting was orchestrated, the
music was catchy, the sermon was contemporarily relevant, and
so on. In business terms, everything was tailored to the customer
experience. And so, what kept people coming back was The
Quest's phenomenal seeker sensitivity. The Quest provided a
great customer experience. The church was relaxed, comfortable,
and organized; people experienced pleasure and comfort when
attending The Quest.

KOINONIA

Koinonia (koy-noh-NEE-uh) is a Greek word that is often
translated and understood as "fellowship." However, the New
Testament uses this word a bit differently than we would
normally understand fellowship. The idea of koinonia is not
that people gather together amongst themselves; instead,
koinonia is when people gather together *around* something.

(See 1 Corinthians 1:9.) In other words, koinonia happens when people participate together in something external, something that pulls various individuals together into a common bond. Christian koinonia happens as God calls people of various backgrounds to participate and share in the common yet uniquely powerful Gospel.

This is not to say that it's wrong or bad to do things well in church. There is nothing wrong with clear advertising, well-organized volunteers, clear sermons, and professional-sounding musicians. Making the church comfortable for outsiders and newcomers can be founded on godly motivations. However, any efforts to that end should be challenged and tested by asking what purpose the seeker sensitivity and great customer experience serve.

Even though it was not directly stated, everything The Quest did was aimed at giving attendees a better customer experience than other churches in Midway. A kind of ecclesiastical competition was embedded in their focus on seeker sensitivity and great customer experience; their desire was not solely to serve a new, unchurched attendee. That is to say, The Quest had the best website, a modern facility, and the best musicians in town—and every churchgoer in Midway knew it. The Quest had grown substantially because it attracted members away from many other long-standing churches. Indeed, the majority of its membership came not from new converts to the Christian faith but from former members of other churches in town—like the couple Ben met in the lobby after the service. As a result, many other churches in Midway harbored an unspoken antagonism toward The Quest, even as they felt pressure to duplicate and mimic The Quest. In fact, one church in Midway had changed its name to "The Voyage" to be more relevant.

• • • • • • • • • • • • • • • • • • • •

That afternoon, after lunch at a local diner, Ben, Jessica, Noah, and Olivia returned home. Noah asked if it was okay to play video games, and Olivia requested to go in the backyard on a swing, which gave Ben and Jessica a few moments to chat while doing dishes left over from Saturday.

"So what did you think of The Quest?" Jessica asked.

"It was nice," Ben replied. "The kids seemed to enjoy it. I know you liked the coffee. What did you think?"

Jessica scrunched up her face, considering the question as she dried a plate. "I don't know. It was good, but . . . it just seemed to be *too* good, you know? We've had a lot of tough Sunday mornings, and this certainly was not one of them. But something just seemed to be missing."

Ben's phone began to ring in his back pocket. Hands dripping with suds, he motioned to Jessica to take the phone out of his pocket. The call was from Ben's parents.

"Hey there. This is Jess. Ben has his hands full with dishes," Jessica said with a giggle.

Ben's parents would often call just to check in. They were wondering if Ben was ready to start his new job on Monday and to see how the family was adjusting.

Jessica shared fun details about the family and mentioned their visit to The Quest.

"Yes, things went well this morning," Jessica said. "Yes, we got there on time. . . . Well, they had some really good coffee, Olivia made a neat hat, and Ben liked the padded chairs. . . . Ha! I'm not sure about Noah. He didn't really say much other than he liked the movie poster. I thought the music was good. What's that? . . . Oh, the movie poster was for the movie the pastor preached about. Have you seen *Deception Friday*?"

• • • • • • • • • • • • • • • • • • •

Indeed, something was missing from The Quest. The purpose of the church was circular; their quest led only to more questing. And at the center of the church was seeker sensitivity and good customer experience. It was no accident that Jessica highlighted the good customer experience when Ben's parents asked, because that is what The Quest clearly focused on as a strength and a reason to keep coming back. When people talk about a church, business, or restaurant, they will often highlight what the entity is known for—what is at the center of the entity. They will often emphasize what keeps people coming back for more. In this case, The Quest attempted to lead the Campbells on an unending journey while making them comfortable and happy, like a luxury cruise to nowhere.

The Quest may have been accommodating, extremely organized, and contemporarily relevant, but Jessica was right. Something seemed to be missing.

Chapter 1 Study Guide

REVIEW

1. What unites the members of The Quest?
2. What is the purpose of The Quest?
3. How did the architecture, floor plans, furnishings, sights, and sounds convey the unity and purpose of The Quest?

DISCUSS

1. Why is it important to know the end goal—the purpose—of the church?
2. How does the center of the church influence the services, members, and church leadership?
3. Why do you think the children were separated from Ben and Jessica? Should children be separated from their parents in church? Does this strengthen or weaken the family?
4. Why does a church like The Quest need to base a sermon on a movie? What are the dangers of doing this?

REFLECT

1. Jessica said that something was missing from The Quest. What is missing?

Parkside Community Fellowship Church

"We won't miss this week," Ben exclaimed as he looked over his shoulder to back out of the driveway.

Laughing, Jessica responded, "I can't believe we all overslept last week for church."

Even though the Campbells had had a very busy week, Noah and Olivia were in good moods and a bit excited to check out a new church, recommended by the mom of Noah's new neighborhood friend, Ethan.

"So I think I know where this church is at, but what is it called again?" Ben questioned as he shifted from reverse to drive.

"Park something," Jessica said, thinking back to the conversation with Ethan's mom.

"It's Parkside Community Fellowship!" Noah interrupted from the back seat. "Ethan isn't going to be there, though. They're camping."

Approximately eleven minutes later, the Campbells approached Parkside Community Fellowship Church. The church was in a planned community called Parkside. All the houses around the church had very similar architecture. The church was a standalone building directly across the street from a small strip mall with a couple of restaurants, a small grocery store, and a small gas station. Diagonally across from the church was a city park with swing sets, picnic benches, and a short walking path.

"Is this it?" Ben asked as he slowed down the vehicle.

"Yes, it must be," Jessica replied, looking out the window at a sign anchored to two white posts with a flower bed around it and "Parkside Community Fellowship Church" written in large text. Underneath it, smaller text in a childlike font read "Pathway Preschool."

Ben eased into the parking lot.

"What is that?" Noah asked, pointing to a larger, box-looking building attached to the church. The larger structure appeared to be newer and added to the original church.

"Probably a gymnasium, bud," answered Ben.

Several minutes later, after the Campbells had parked their SUV next to several minivans, they began walking toward the church entrance. At first, it was difficult to discern which door to enter. To the left was a shorter building, which appeared to be the church sanctuary. However, the larger building to the right had newer and wider sidewalks as well as a more manicured lawn with fresh flowers. As the Campbells approached the sidewalk, it became obvious that they should enter to the right; two other families had just walked in that way.

Just like at The Quest, the Campbells began to smell the aroma of coffee as they entered the larger building. However, instead of high energy and anticipation, the Campbells found themselves in a multipurpose gym full of smiles, laughter, and young children running around. The floors were carpeted, and one side was filled with round white tables where people were drinking coffee and eating bakery rolls. The Campbells surveyed the room, and Ben made eye contact with a man who looked to be in his late fifties. The man smiled and walked their way.

"Good morning. I'm Pastor Dan. You can just call me Dan." He extended his hand for a handshake. After exchanging introductions, Pastor Dan said, "Let me show you around the church. I have about ten minutes to spare before the service begins."

Pastor Dan started by showing the Campbells the gym, the newest addition to the church. He beamed as he shared that it was for Sunday fellowship and a variety of weekly activities, from gym time for their preschool to youth dodgeball on Wednesday nights, a women's yoga class on Thursday, and an open gym for men's basketball on Saturday mornings.

Pastor Dan added, "Here at Parkside, we don't believe in the church sitting empty the other six and a half days a week. We really want everyone in the church to be active and feel like this place is their home. Think of Parkside as a home away from home—a safe place to gather that is set apart from the busy and difficult world."

CHURCH BUILDING LAYOUT

In the past, most churches only had a sanctuary and a small narthex (that is, an entryway). If they were lucky, they may have had a basement. Apart from regularly scheduled church services, the parishioners' Monday-through-Saturday life did not occur within the four walls of the church facility. So if there were no gyms, fellowship halls, lobbies, cafes, courtyards, or multipurpose rooms, where did the Christians practice their faith the other six days of the week? It occurred in their vocations. It happened in the estate of the family. (See Titus 2:1–15; Ephesians 5:21–6:9.)

After walking through the gymnasium, Pastor Dan took the Campbells to the north wing of the church complex to see the Pathway Preschool. Pastor Dan shared his excitement about the preschool—how the preschool was a great part of the church in attracting new members. He shared how his vision was to expand the preschool to an elementary school and then, in the future, to a private Christian high school.

They continued working their way through the halls of the preschool wing until Pastor Dan pulled them off to another room. "I just love this space," he said. "We call it our fireside room."

A large electric fireplace was at the center of the room, with couches surrounding it. Bookshelves on the walls held board games, movies, and books. There were also tables set up throughout the room, along with a small kitchen.

"Feels just like home, doesn't it?" Pastor Dan asserted.

The room indeed felt like a living room at a house, with quality furniture and tasteful decorating.

"So what is this room used for?" Ben asked.

"Well, we use it for just about everything, from our small-group Bible studies to our parenting classes to our moms' group," Pastor Dan replied. "Pretty much every adult group in the church uses this room, if they aren't in the gym." Looking at his watch, he leaned forward and spoke with excitement, "Let me show you one more thing, and then I will take you to the sanctuary."

As the Campbells walked with him, they approached large sheets of construction plastic hanging from the ceiling.

"Please excuse the mess," Pastor Dan said, holding up the plastic sheet so they could enter the large room. "This is our new youth group room. It isn't done yet, but this will soon be a place for our youth to come for youth group and to hang out."

Not believing what she was seeing, Jessica interrupted, "Is that a bowling lane?"

Pastor Dan laughed and said, "Yes, it is. One of the parents offered to pay for a bowling lane in the youth room—so why not? Like the fireside room, this youth room will have a small kitchen, a sound system, and plenty of room for couches. We are also adding vending machines and some locker space over on the west side so that people have a place to change and shower before and after the gym activities. We hope this room will not only help with the youth group but also draw our youth to the church throughout the week."

Looking at his watch again, Pastor Dan chuckled. "Wow, church is starting in two minutes. Oh well, here at Parkside, sometimes services start late when we get carried away in our fellowship!"

FRIENDSHIP VERSUS FELLOWSHIP

Friendship and biblical fellowship are different. Friendship is a direct connection and bond between individuals who enjoy one another's company. We might picture friendship as two dots connected directly to each other by a line. Biblical fellowship is more than just friendship among Christians. Rather than connecting similar people through bonds of friendship, biblical fellowship connects many dissimilar people through Christ's life, death, and resurrection. Picture biblical fellowship as a wheel, where spokes connect individual dots to a common, central point that holds them together—Christ. While friendship is certainly a blessing, biblical fellowship unites people of all backgrounds, ages, and ethnicities in Christ, despite any social, economic, or cultural differences that would otherwise make friendship difficult. (See 1 Corinthians 1:9.)

Pastor Dan led the Campbells to the sanctuary and then left to prepare for the service. A warm and friendly couple standing at the sanctuary doors handed a bulletin to each Campbell as they entered.

"I guess they didn't get around to updating this part yet," Ben whispered to Jessica, looking around at the space.

The sanctuary wasn't old by any means, but compared to the gym, preschool, and youth room, it didn't seem as well maintained. The ceiling felt particularly low after they had been in the high-ceilinged gymnasium. Long pews stretched horizontally across the wide room, facing the stage at the front that held a small wooden podium and a small altar.

The family shuffled into a pew on the left side and sat down.

"It's nice to sit together, isn't it?" Jessica said, giving Olivia a quick squeeze around the shoulders. After getting situated, Jessica looked up and noticed that people on the right side of the sanctuary were looking at them. They smiled at her for a brief second and seemed friendly, just like everyone else at Parkside, but Jessica was caught off guard.

"What's up?" Ben asked, noticing her reaction.

"Oh, I just wasn't expecting to be able to see the people across the sanctuary," she replied.

Ben looked around then, too, and saw that the pews were actually in a U shape around the front of the church, so that people on the edges could see those worshiping across from them.

"Maybe next time we should sit in the middle toward the back so we can be more anonymous," Jessica said quietly.

Ben smiled, nodded his head, and put his arm around her.

SANCTUARY ARCHITECTURE

Church architecture is more than just a design choice. In fact, the architecture of a sanctuary communicates things about God, reverence, and mankind. Think about the differences between a sanctuary that is wide and low and one that is long and tall. Picture yourself in a wide, low sanctuary, where the most people are arranged to your sides around a small altar. Where do your eyes travel—up and down or left and right? How do you speak—quietly or loudly? How do you feel—casual or reverential? Now consider those questions again, but picture yourself in a long sanctuary with a high ceiling and a large altar, where everyone is facing the front together.

The quick answer is that church sanctuaries that are longer and taller tend to direct members' attention forward and up—typically to a cross or altar. However, churches with lower and wider sanctuaries tend to direct the attention of members around the space, toward one another. In spaces like these, churches would need to find other ways to keep the cross and altar as the main focal point.

As Ben looked toward the stage, he noticed that Parkside had a praise-and-worship band. However, it was quite different from The Quest. Instead of being center stage, the instruments were off to the left side, allowing everyone to still see a simple wooden cross on the wall above the altar. Ben realized that he had not seen a cross displayed anywhere at The Quest.

After a few minutes of prelude music, Pastor Dan came walking in from the back of the church. He had put on a tie and sports jacket, looking a bit more formal than when he had given a tour to the Campbells.

"Welcome to Parkside, where we love God and one another," Pastor Dan shared.

Even though the service had started late, it was obvious that many people were still making their way into the sanctuary; the sounds of warm conversation filtered in from outside the sanctuary doors. Pastor Dan then directed everyone to the bulletin announcements.

Ben and Jessica exchanged a glance, eyebrows raised, as they looked at the announcements. Pastor Dan had not been kidding when he talked about people using the church building throughout the week; every day and night was filled with activity. Even though it was smaller than The Quest, Parkside Community Fellowship Church had twice as many small groups and activities throughout the week.

During the next fifteen minutes of announcements, the Campbells heard not only from Pastor Dan but also from six other church leaders about upcoming events. On Tuesday, there was a pool party behind the church for children Olivia's age, with popcorn and a Bible memory game. On Wednesday, there was dodgeball, pizza, and a Bible devotional for youth around Noah's age. Both Noah and Olivia looked excitedly at their parents as they heard about the fun activities. Jessica smiled at them before directing her attention back to the speaker, who was now sharing several opportunities for Ben and Jessica to get involved in parenting classes, cooking clubs, and date-night devotions.

CHURCH SCHEDULES AND MONASTERIES

Many of us believe monasteries are things of the past—relics from the medieval period—but, surprisingly, they are popping up all around us and have been for some time. That is to say, many churches in the United States have become modern-day monasteries. The constant stream of activities—and the gyms and large fellowship halls that house them—takes Christians out of society and walls them inside church facilities throughout the week. And while the rest of the church facility bustles with activity the other six days of the week, the sanctuary lies dormant, still used just one day a week for services. In other words, large segments of Christianity conduct nearly all of their social lives and interactions only within the four walls of the church facility. (See John 17:11.)

Eventually, the church service started. It consisted of music from the praise band, Scripture readings, a testimonial time from a member, and a sermon preached by Pastor Dan from the floor in front of the first pew. He spoke about how the world outside would continue to get darker but emphasized that within the walls of Parkside Community Fellowship, everyone could walk together to create a positive little corner in the world while being accountable to one another.

After some prayers and another song, Pastor Dan stood back up, dismissed the church, and said, "I look forward to seeing you all out in the gym after this!"

"Is that the end? Can we get lunch now?" Noah asked.

"I think so, bud," Ben replied, a little surprised at the short service length. It had been longer than the announcements, but not by much.

The worshipers began filing out of the sanctuary through the large doors that led to the gym. The hum of conversation started back up as the Campbells moved slowly through the line. Ben noticed Pastor Dan standing near the gym doors, shaking hands with everyone, clearly chatting with each family for a while.

"Do you think we could just leave out that door?" Jessica asked hesitantly, pointing to the sanctuary doors that exited to the parking lot rather than the gym.

Ben shrugged and looked around to see if anyone else was exiting that way. As he did so, he made eye contact with the member behind them in line.

"Hey, is it okay if we exit through these doors?" Ben asked, then flinched when he realized he hadn't introduced himself. "Sorry, my name is Ben, and this is my wife, Jessica. We are new here."

The member smiled and reached out his hand. "Great to meet you, Ben and Jessica. You can certainly use that door, but Pastor Dan likes everyone to go in and out of the gym as our main entrance."

Confused, Ben said, "Sorry, I am not quite understanding."

Nodding his head kindly, the member explained, "Pastor Dan doesn't want people using the sanctuary door because he wants members to connect with one another in the gym. He doesn't want people to be 'loner' Christians, to zip in and out of the church. He wants everyone to be plugged in to the life of the church and not be eager to leave the church family and get back to life outside. Here at Parkside, the church is neither home nor work but a place that provides safe fellowship."

· · · · · · · · · · · · · · · · · · · ·

The Campbells learned a lot about Parkside's architecture, scheduling, and focus during the ninety minutes they were at the church. Parkside Community Fellowship Church had a nice church facility and was extremely welcoming. However, our two original questions need to be addressed: What is the purpose of Parkside Community Fellowship Church? What unites it?

SECTARIANISM

Sectarianism is placing a large distance between ourselves and the world. We recognize that the world is hostile to Christ and His Word. We recognize that we don't belong to the world, so we remove ourselves from the world. We dig a moat around ourselves. We fortify the walls. We keep the world "out there" and keep us safe "in here." While it is true that Christians are not "of" the world, we must not forget that we are still "in" the world. (See John 17:11–18.)

First, let us examine the purpose of Parkside Community Fellowship Church: where did the church's architecture, scheduling, and actions point the Campbells? Perhaps the comment by the anonymous member in line at the end of the service helps answer our first question.

For the Campbells to be truly plugged in to the church body, they would have needed to spend a lot of time in the gym, preschool, and fireside room. The schedule, architecture, and emphasis on friendship connections pointed the Campbells not only away from the sanctuary but also away from any events and activities that occurred outside of the church's extensive fellowship facilities. Parkside's focus was on creating their own safe haven, an alternative culture to the world's distractions. In other words, their purpose was to become sectarian or monastic.

VOCATION

The word *vocation* refers to the particular offices, tasks, or roles that God works through to care for His creation. God cares for children through parents; He fixes cars through mechanics; He protects through police officers; He heals through doctors, and so on. Thus, vocations require Christians to interact with the world as they serve in those roles and tasks. In their vocations, they serve their neighbor in need. While Christians are not of the world, they are certainly in the world as they serve others as teachers, mechanics, police officers, doctors, and so on. (See Ephesians 2:10; 6:5-9.)

While parishioners must certainly be at the church to maintain the building, conduct needed business, make plans, and attend church services, most of the Christian's piety will be played out in their God-given vocations. In other words, the church is not an escape from one's vocations as parent, child, worker, citizen, and the like. Instead, the church is the one place where Christians gather to be forgiven of their failures, strengthened in faith, and built up in love *so that they can joyfully leave* the four walls of the church and serve others in their vocations, walking in the good works that God has prepared for them in advance (see Ephesians 2:10). But when the activities of Christians occur exclusively in churches, the church becomes a modern-day monastery.

A monastery provides a safe, secluded world for people to focus on their piety. Tragically, in monastic-minded churches, parishioners can become inward-focused, and their vocations in the "real world" are often neglected. Monastic-minded churches set themselves up to be secluded safehouses, which means that Christian good works are not flowing outward into vocations but staying within the church's walls. Churches are not meant to be monasteries, and the health of the local church should not necessarily be tied to the religious fervor or bustle inside the walls of the church.

Does this mean that churches should not be active or busy? By no means! As we will learn in future chapters, the health of any local church is instead tied to the distribution and reception of the Word and Sacraments. Healthy Christians come to the church often and regularly to receive—to be strengthened in their faith in God and built up in love for their neighbors. Any busyness, religious fervor, and bustle inside the church walls should be about receiving, not doing. We receive from the church (i.e., faith); we serve our neighbors in our vocations (i.e., love). Christians come to church not to give their best to God but to receive God's best in Christ so that they may continually be strengthened and built up in the truth and be able to serve their neighbors in love.

Now we turn to our second question: What united Parkside Community Fellowship Church? Despite the church's name, the answer is friendship. Fellowship requires a central thing in common around which people unite, but the members at Parkside were united by maintaining friendship connections as they gathered throughout the week and participated together in the activities of the church.

Churches are not going deep enough when they base unity on friendships, common experiences, similar opinions, and warm feelings of acceptance. That is to say, if a church unites only through friendship, then the unity is only as strong as the relationships. What happens when collective experiences and feelings reach a point of contention and disagreement? A unity based on friendships, experiences, feelings, and opinions alone is fragile at best. We do not have to look far to see entire churches destroyed by disagreements over nonessential things.

If our relationships in the church are not true fellowship, rooted deeply in Christ Jesus, then small social conflicts can easily destroy the church's unity. Otherwise stated, if the various activities of the church do not uphold and support the church's services, where everyone is united around Christ—together in one voice, one confession, and complete unity—then they are divisive at best and unchristian at worst. The fact is that friendships come and go. If our friends stop being entertaining, enjoyable, and encouraging, we may decide to find new friends. And if we can't find new friends in the church, well, we may break unity with the church and seek friends elsewhere. Sadly, our relationships are not as strong as we tend to believe, and we humans are often superficial. And so, if a church's unity is based upon these fragile relationships, then it has been built upon shifting sands rather than the solid foundation—mere friendship rather than true fellowship.

• • • • • • • • • • • • • • • • • • •

Later that evening, the Campbells were getting ready for their Monday routines. Jessica was excited, as it was her turn to start her new job as a dental hygienist.

"Mom, do I get to go swimming this week at the church?" Olivia asked with excitement.

Pulling out the most famous parent line ever, Jessica responded, "We'll see, sweetie. It is time for bed."

Noah, overhearing the conversation, jumped in. "I really want to go to dodgeball too."

Ben stepped in and replied, "Your mom is right. We will see," and sent both kids off to bed.

Once the kids were asleep, Jessica turned to Ben as they rested on the couch together. "What are we going to do about the pool party on Tuesday and dodgeball on Wednesday?"

Ben sighed. "I get that the kids are excited, and the church did have a lot of activities. But I guess I never thought that we had to be that busy in a church to be fully plugged in."

Nodding her head, Jessica replied, "I have no idea how we could swing everything with a church schedule that busy. We're already busy enough with the new jobs and the kids' activities, and you know it will only get busier once school starts in the fall."

After a brief pause in the conversation, Ben looked over at Jessica. "Pastor Dan was a super nice guy, and the people were very friendly, but something seemed to be missing."

Chapter 2 Study Guide

REVIEW

1. What unites the members of Parkside Community Fellowship Church?
2. What is the purpose of Parkside Community Fellowship Church?
3. How did the architecture, floor plans, furnishings, sights, and sounds convey the unity and purpose of Parkside Community Fellowship Church?

DISCUSS

1. Have you ever thought about how church architecture and building layout can communicate the purpose of a local church?
2. What does a monastic approach offer churchgoers?
3. Why could a focus on friendship prove detrimental to a church's foundation?
4. The chapter stated, "Churches are not meant to be monasteries, and the health of the local church should not necessarily be tied to the religious fervor or bustle inside the walls of the church." Do you agree or disagree?

REFLECT

1. Ben said that something seemed to be missing from Parkside. What is missing?

Mercy Hill Church

This Sunday morning found the Campbells driving through the narrow streets of Midway's historic downtown, passing various local diners, antique shops, and boutiques on their way to a new church.

"There sure are a lot of people out and about," Ben commented as he stopped at a crosswalk for some elderly pedestrians.

"Yes. Didn't our real estate agent say that a lot of Midway's population lives around here?" Jessica replied, looking out the window at the bustle of diners, business owners, and window-shoppers next to the SUV. "I think she said there were several subsidized apartment buildings in the old downtown for low-income families and those with disabilities, and a lot of studios for college students and singles."

"That's right. Oh, this must be it," Ben said as he pulled into a tiny parking lot between a church and a hardware store.

"What beautiful stained glass windows," Jessica declared.

Mercy Hill Church was a mainline church in the heart of Midway's old downtown district, several blocks from the main commuter railway. The church's architecture was stunning, and the slightly elevated lot made the steeple stand out amid the downtown skyline.

MAINLINE CHURCHES

"Mainline churches" are a group of historic Protestant churches in the United States. According to some historians, the term *mainline* stems from the fact that many of the Protestant churches in Philadelphia were located along the Main Line of the Pennsylvania Railroad.

"Dad, what is that building?" Noah asked.

Ben looked where Noah was pointing, taking a moment to examine the structure extending off the back of the church. "I'm not quite sure, Son."

"Noah, I think it is a soup kitchen or a food pantry," Jessica said. "That sign says 'Heaven's Helpers,' and it has a little picture of soup and vegetables."

HISTORY OF SOUP KITCHENS

During the Great Depression in the 1930s, many Americans were out of work. To help, soup kitchens dramatically expanded to meet the basic needs of American families. Soup kitchens developed in every city and town, offering bread and soup through the work of private charities, volunteers, and churches. Today, many soup kitchens have continued and now also offer clothing, hygiene kits, and various staple foods.

The Campbell family walked past a wide handicap ramp to climb up several flights of stairs to enter the church. In the small narthex, Olivia noticed several rows of backpacks. Some were on the floor. Others were hanging on hooks. Seeing one in particular, Olivia smiled.

"Mom, look! That backpack is just like mine!"

Jessica paused for a second and looked at the wall, confused about why there would be so many backpacks in one place. The ushers at the door must have seen the Campbells looking at the backpack wall, and one came over to greet them.

"Good morning," an usher said while handing a bulletin to Jessica. "Make yourself at home." He motioned for the Campbells to sit down in the sanctuary. Thankfully, there was an open pew on the right side. Ben gestured to the kids to sit in the empty pew.

The sanctuary was moderately filled with a mixture of young and old. The pews seemed aged, maybe solid oak. The stained glass windows were even more beautiful from the inside, casting various colors toward the front of the church, where an old altar, lectern, and pulpit were situated. The ornaments and decorations on the altar, lectern, and pulpit were also quite vibrant in color. Long, multicolored banners hung from tall pillars and displayed the words *diversity, justice, mercy,* and *harmony.*

MINISTRIES OR MINISTRY?

Over the years, there has been the sentiment that everyone is a minister. While it is true that through the church's ministry, pastors and Christians proclaim the Gospel to a dying world, it is not valid that everything the church and the Christian does in the name of God is a ministry. In fact, there is only one ministry: the proclamation of the Gospel and the distribution of God's sacramental gifts. But how should activism, good works, and humanitarian endeavors be considered? They should be thought of as activism, good works, and humanitarian endeavors: they are acts of love, mercy, and help toward suffering neighbors. And so, the church has one ministry—the Gospel—and many different ways to serve others in need with acts of love and mercy. (See 1 Corinthians 4:1; Ephesians 4:11–12; Acts 20:28.)

As Ben and Jessica looked through the bulletin, the minister walked in from the back of the sanctuary. She was wearing a plain white linen robe with a colorful band of silk hanging around her neck. As she reached the front, she turned and faced the church, saying, "Good morning, brothers and sisters. Welcome to Mercy Hill, where we are God's hands and feet."

The rest of the church responded in unison, "Good morning."

The minister then took several minutes to highlight the church bulletin. She briefly mentioned a couple of groups in the church that were meeting throughout the week. Then she took a little extra time to say, "On Wednesday, we want to invite all of you to come to the church to help restock the food pantry, clean up the soup kitchen, and finish packing the preschool backpacks. These are vital ministries at Mercy Hill, and we need every helping hand."

The service continued with several traditional and contemporary hymns, Scripture readings, and a short sermon on the importance of loving one's neighbor. In the sermon, the minister encouraged the congregation to preach the Gospel at all times and, if necessary, to use words. She quoted this sentiment several times and attributed it to St. Francis of Assisi, emphasizing how the members of Mercy Hill could fulfill Jesus' Great Commission as they "embodied the Gospel." She stressed the need for the members to "be the Gospel" to a neighbor in need by meeting basic human needs in the name of Jesus.

GREAT COMMISSION VERSUS GREAT COMMANDMENT

Despite their similar names, the Great Commission (Matthew 28:18-20) and the Great Commandment are very different (Matthew 22:36-40). Here are a few examples:

The Great Commandment is about serving neighbors through loving works.

CHAPTER 3 | MERCY HILL CHURCH

The Great Commission is about making disciples through the Gospel.

The Great Commandment put into words says, "I love you."

The Great Commission says, "Let me tell you about God's love for you in the life, death, and resurrection of Jesus Christ."

The Great Commandment consists of good deeds that we do for our neighbor.

The Great Commission consists of a good message about what God did for the world.

What this distinction shows is that Christians cannot "be" the Gospel, for the Gospel is an external message found outside of the Christian. The Gospel is not the actions and deeds of the Christian but the actions and deeds of Christ for the Christian. Therefore, serving soup, packing backpacks, and the like are not fulfilling the Great Commission; instead, they are doing the Great Commandment.

As Christians, though, we do not have an either-or decision, as if we have to choose between the Great Commission and the Great Commandment. No, we are invited into both: to tell our neighbor about Jesus and to love our neighbor by serving them and meeting their needs.

Following the sermon, the minister said, "At this time, we will we take our offering."

Ben reached into his back pocket to grab his wallet, but then he noticed ushers walking up the aisles with backpacks in their hands. The backpacks were placed at the foot of the altar. As the ushers situated the backpacks, other individuals passed offering plates back and forth through the pews. As the plate came to the pew the Campbells were sitting in, Olivia motioned to her dad. She wanted to place the crisp fifty-dollar bill into the offering plate.

After the offering plates were returned to the front altar, the minister asked the congregation to rise, saying, "I ask anyone who has backpack supplies to please bring them to the front."

About 60 percent of the congregation made their way to the front of the church. Before the altar, the church members laid a variety of groceries: cereal boxes, canned peaches, granola bars, jerky, fruit snacks, and so on. Once the last grocery item was placed by the backpacks, the minister closed her eyes.

"Let us pray. Dear God, bless these grocery gifts that they may feed Your people. May we continue to be Your hands and feet in this place and at this time through our backpack ministry. Amen. Please be seated."

TITHING

In the Old Testament, families were expected to give three tithes, which were then dispersed to the Levites, to the festival meals, and to the widows, orphans, and poor strangers. (See Leviticus 27:30-33; Deuteronomy 14:22-29.) The three tithes totaled approximately 22 percent of income. In the New Testament church, offerings were allocated to support Christian workers, mission work, and humanitarian help. (See 1 Corinthians 9:13-18; Romans 15:24; Titus 3:13; Acts 11:29-30.)

After the service, the Campbells gathered their things and headed to the back of the sanctuary. The minister was shaking hands as people left.

"Good morning. You must be new here. I'm Pastor Brandy," she said.

Ben and Jessica introduced themselves and explained that they were new to the area. Since the line behind them was relatively short, Pastor Brandy was not rushed and asked them several more questions.

Motioning to the altar at the front, Jessica asked, "So are the backpacks today for a certain preschool or a certain group of children?" She had been a bit confused by that part during the service, though it seemed that the groceries and backpacks were being given to children in need.

Nodding her head, Pastor Brandy answered, "Yes, each week we fill backpacks for children in need. Then on Fridays, we bring them to the Washington Early Childhood Center. It is a voluntary prekindergarten program here in Midway that provides free and discounted preschool. They give us more empty backpacks when we do the drop-off on Fridays, and then we fill those for the next week. During the school year, we partner with several other churches in Midway and fill backpacks for grade school children as well."

Both Ben and Jessica were rather impressed by the devotion with which Pastor Brandy spoke.

She went on to say, "Here at Mercy Hill, we have been feeding the hungry and helping the poor for over a hundred years. Our Heaven's Helpers food pantry is open on Tuesdays and Thursdays. It helps area residents with groceries and clothing. Our soup kitchen serves meals on Mondays, Wednesdays, and Fridays. Most of the families we serve live in one of the subsidized apartment buildings in the area. And some of the people we serve are, unfortunately, homeless. We keep very busy with all of this, and we couldn't do any of it if not for our members."

Pastor Brandy thanked the Campbells for the brief conversation, invited them to the activities on Wednesday, and wished them a pleasant day. It was an enjoyable and kind conversation.

THE THREE ESTATES

The Small Catechism and the Epistle of Titus identify three estates, or spheres, in life: the church, the state, and the family.

Each estate functions differently but is equally necessary for a healthy society. For example, the church gives gifts of grace (i.e., the Gospel). The state bears the sword to maintain order and peace (i.e., law). And the family nurtures and provides (i.e., mercy).

When one of these estates is absent or negligent, however, society will demand that the other two compensate to pick up the slack. As a result, when the church lacks, politicians will be expected to turn their podiums into pulpits and be pastors. When fathers and mothers fail to provide and nurture for their families within the estate of the family, they inevitably put a burden on the church and the state to be parents in their stead. The negligence of the state can cause pastors to turn their pulpits into political podiums, attempting to keep order instead of administering the gifts of God's grace via the Word and Sacraments. In the end, when one estate suffers, all estates suffer.

The church is not designed to bear the sword, just as the state is not designed to deliver the means of grace, and it is not good for the family to neglect its nurturing and provisional care. Each estate is necessary and good for a healthy society.

As the Campbells walked to their car, an older man approached them with a bright smile. Reaching out his hand, he greeted them warmly. "My name is Bill. It is great to see such a nice-looking young family at Mercy Hill."

After several brief introductions of the family, Bill went on to explain the food pantry and soup kitchen that Noah had spotted when they first arrived. "It began with a few of us at church wanting to make a difference. We reached out to local businesses and the community, and people have been so generous with their donations. It's grown so much since we started."

It was obvious that he was an active leader in the church, as he further explained how poverty affects the mind—placing people into survival mode and what he called "time poverty."

The Campbells listened as he continued.

"Imagine not having a safe place to sleep or enough food to eat. It becomes a constant, all-consuming effort to survive. It's tough to focus on education, job opportunities, or personal growth when your main concern is where your next meal will come from or where you'll sleep tonight. Breaking free from poverty often requires not just hard work but also support and resources to meet those basic needs. That is where Mercy Hill comes into the picture.

"Very few of us could make it through a major tragedy on our own," Bill shared compassionately. "We are all very fragile. The only real thing that keeps us afloat is our community, which serves as a backstop. A strong family—which is what we try to be here at Mercy Hill—is the greatest asset a person can have."

Ben and Jessica nodded, thinking of their own supportive parents, before saying their goodbyes to Bill and ushering the kids back to the car.

• • • • • • • • • • • • • • • • • • •

What unifies Mercy Hill Church? What is their driving purpose? Before this can be answered, it is important to understand that in a perfect world, families would always be able to provide for the basic mercy and care of one another and their neighbors. Furthermore, in an ideal world, the government would always honorably work to keep order and justice, while the church would always teach morals and deliver forgiveness. However, life is not perfect: the state fails, churches fail, and families fail as well. Indeed, the family, church, and state often drop the ball, resulting in one of the other estates needing to pick up the slack.

In the case of Mercy Hill, the church has stepped into the estate of the family to provide mercy and care for those in need—those who do not have the support of a family. While providing mercy and care is honorable and good, that is not the main and exclusive purpose of the church. Instead, mercy and care belong to the estate of the family. And so, to answer the question of what unites Mercy Hill's members, it would be that Mercy Hill Church and its members stand in the void for those who have broken families. Furthermore, the purpose of Mercy Hill Church is to provide for the basic physiological needs of food, water, and clothing to individuals who are not obtaining basic needs from the estate of the family. Succinctly stated, Mercy Hill Church is unified in standing in the void of family for the purpose of providing mercy and care.

Is Mercy Hill Church out of line? No, it is not. In both the Old and New Testaments, we read countless passages where the faithful are called to show mercy to those in need. For example, in Leviticus 23:22, the Israelites were instructed to give crop provisions to the poor and sojourners; in 1 Timothy 5:13–16, Paul gives instructions on giving help to widows and so forth. Historically, the church has been concerned with the poor, needy, and weak within the church. And during times of great disaster, the church has always seemed to reach outside its walls to help those in need. However, the primary function of the estate of the church lies elsewhere. By uniting around a task that is meant for another estate, Mercy Hill loses sight of what the church is rightly called to do.

Throughout the history of the Christian Church, much of the social work (caring for widows, orphans, and the poor) was done by Christians. Such care was typically not officially organized by the church but happened as Christians served their neighbors in need through the estate of the family. This does not diminish the importance of the church; rather, it shows how the Christians' faith influenced them to engage in society and effect change through their various positive individual actions.

• • • • • • • • • • • • • • • • • • • •

After church, the Campbells went for lunch at Thai Delight, which had become their new favorite family restaurant. Ben loved their pad thai, while Jessica craved the pad see ew. Noah and Olivia always shared a large order of fried rice with eggs, vegetables, and chicken.

"That was pretty amazing at Mercy Hill, wasn't it?" Ben said after he had taken a few bites. He looked down at his plate, feeling a little guilty for eating delicious Thai food after hearing about all the individuals in Midway who experienced hunger pains.

Nodding her head, Jess replied, "It was really impressive. They seemed very organized."

Ben finished chewing another bite and looked over at the kids. "What did you both think of the church?"

Noah, in his usual fashion, replied, "It was cool, Dad."

Olivia was excited, though. "I think it is really neat how they help so many people. I like that," she said. "Are we going to go there again?"

Hesitating, Jessica answered, "You know, let's do this. They seem to be very busy on Wednesdays with their soup kitchen and food pantry. Perhaps we could go help on Wednesdays from time to time."

Olivia scrunched her face. "Didn't you like the church, Mommy?"

Taken aback a bit, Jessica replied, "Oh, sweetie, yes, I really liked the church. It was a good church. They are doing some really good things to help people."

Looking up from his food, Noah asked, "So why wouldn't we go back?"

This time, Ben answered. "I think what your mom is getting at is that we could help the church out on Wednesdays, but maybe we could keep looking—"

"But why would we keep looking?" Olivia asked, interrupting her dad.

After a short pause, Jessica gently replied, "Because the church is not just a food pantry or soup kitchen. There must be something more, sweetie."

Chapter 3 Study Guide

REVIEW

1. What unites the members of Mercy Hill Church?
2. What is the purpose of Mercy Hill Church?
3. How did the architecture, floor plans, furnishings, sights, and sounds convey the unity and purpose of Mercy Hill Church?

DISCUSS

1. If you had to write a mission statement for Mercy Hill Church, what would it say?
2. Do you agree with Mercy Hill Church's pastor that we should preach the Gospel at all times, and if necessary, use words?
3. How would you describe the difference between the Great Commandment and the Great Commission?
4. How would you describe the three estates to a member at Mercy Hill Church?

REFLECT

1. Jessica told Olivia, "The church is not just a food pantry or soup kitchen. There must be something more." What more is needed at Mercy Hill Church?

First Church of Midway

A couple of weeks had passed since the Campbells attended Mercy Hill Church. They had hit the road for a small family vacation over the Fourth of July. Though the family was not too big on the outdoors, they nonetheless enjoyed a bit of camping with a small pop-up camper they borrowed from Ben's parents. They had decided to sleep in on the Sunday they were out of town. Today, though, they were back to trying to find a new church home.

"What's the name of this church again that Dr. Philips told you about?" asked Ben.

Dr. Mark Philips was Jessica's boss and the owner of the dental practice she worked at. He and his wife, Cathy, were longtime residents of Midway. They both grew up in Midway and attended the same high school together. Cathy worked in the dental front office, and she would often recount high school memories from forty years ago with her coworkers. Apparently, Mark had been the quarterback for the Midway Mustangs, and Cathy, full of team spirit, had led the cheerleading squad.

"First Church of Midway. It's just east of Mercy Hill, across the river in the new downtown portion," Jessica answered.

On their way to First Church of Midway, the Campbells drove right past Mercy Hill Church. Ben found himself nodding in approval as he looked out his window at the beautiful old church—the kind of nod that shows respect. Even though something had seemed to be missing from Mercy Hill, he still appreciated the work they were doing.

As Ben drove over a small double-beam drawbridge, First Church of Midway came into view. Two impressive steeples with clocks embedded into the red brick rose four or five stories high, standing out above the buildings of the new downtown.

Ben drove slowly past the church, looking for a place to park. The church appeared to be old, though it seemed newer than Mercy Hill. However, a lot of money had clearly gone into the church building. There were several small additions, and the main structure had been very well maintained, with clean white pillars holding up ornate archways over the doors.

"What's that place?" Olivia said from the back seat while pointing to a building across the street from the church.

"That must be city hall," Jessica answered. "Look over there, Olivia. That house next to city hall is the mayoral mansion."

Noah looked then too. "A mansion? Really?"

With a bit of a chuckle, Ben said, "It is not really a mansion. I am sure it was one of the biggest houses in Midway when it was built, but it's not anymore."

Finally, Ben saw a small sign with arrows that said "Additional Church Parking," directing them to what appeared to be the parking lot for the district court building kitty-corner from the church.

"Are you sure we can park here?" Jessica questioned.

"It appears so," Ben remarked, nodding toward several well-dressed people exiting sparkling luxury cars.

As the Campbells crossed the street and approached the church, it was even more impressive than they had seen from their SUV. They walked up the outside stairs of the church and were greeted by several ushers handing out bulletins. The ushers were kind and friendly but not overly accommodating.

Once the church service began, it was evident that the choir, pastor, and accompanist were professional. The service style was drastically different from The Quest, but First Church of Midway was just as organized and finely tuned.

Jessica found her mind wandering a bit during the service. Parts of First Church of Midway reminded her of the various other churches they had attended lately. From the bulletin, she saw that First Church of Midway was involved in humanitarian endeavors, much like Mercy Hill Church. First Church of Midway also seemed to have activities going on throughout the week, like Parkside Community Fellowship. And like The Quest, First Church of Midway was clearly well polished and organized. However, even though parts of it were similar to the other churches, the overall atmosphere was drastically different.

When the service ended, Ben reached to put the hymnal back in the slot on the pew in front of him. He fumbled it, and the hymnal fell open, a few pages bending as he kept it from dropping. Jessica looked over with a half-smile, her expression clearly communicating, "You are lucky you didn't make a scene, buddy." Ben grinned back, closing the hymnal meticulously as if to say, "I've got this." As he did so, he noticed a stamp on the inside cover that said, "Given in loving memory of Ruth Archer."

As the Campbells waited to leave their pew, Jessica saw Dr. Philips and Cathy ahead of them, about to shake hands with the pastor. Cathy waved at Jessica and then made a hand motion to indicate that they could meet down the hall.

GIVING WALLS

A "giving wall" is a creative way to display donations to an organization, usually in an effort to recognize the generosity of certain donors. Such displays usually categorize donations based on amount and feature different tiers that are easily distinguished on sight. For example, a gold-colored sign for the top givers, silver for the next, and bronze after that. (See Matthew 6:3-4.)

The Campbells walked down the hallway that Cathy had motioned to, with a sign indicating that they were headed toward the fellowship hall. Various gold, silver, and bronze plaques lined the hallway. Jessica looked a little closer and realized it was a giving wall. Each plaque signified a certain amount of donations to the church. Some were quite large.

As at Parkside Community Fellowship Church, the noise increased as they approached the fellowship hall.

"Look," Ben said, pointing to the words above the doors, "*Archer* Fellowship Hall."

Jessica had not seen the inside of the hymnal, though, and did not get the reference.

As Ben started to explain, Cathy's voice rang out, "Jessica, over here!"

Cathy waved them over to where she was standing in a loose circle with her husband and several others. Dr. Philips reached out his hand to Ben as the family approached.

"You must be Ben. I have heard so much about you." Then he shook Jessica's hand and turned to the group. "Everyone, I want to introduce you to Ben and Jessica Campbell. Jessica works for me, and Ben is an up-and-coming CPA here in Midway at Miller and Associates Accounting."

Ben did not really consider himself an up-and-coming certified public accountant in Midway; nonetheless, it felt nice to have a little bit of recognition. Dr. Philips went on to introduce some others in the group: one person was the registrar at Midway State University, another was a state attorney, and another was a small business owner. Most of the people seemed older than Ben and Jessica and were clearly well established in the community. Ben began visiting with people to his right, and Jessica started chatting with some ladies to her left, while Noah and Olivia tried not to look too bored by the adult conversation.

KING OF THE HILL

We do it all the time without even thinking about it: ranking one another. Back in school, we ranked everyone by popularity. The really cool kids were on top, and the not-so-cool kids were at the bottom. As we get older, we start to rank people on the success of their children, where they live, the size of their house, the type of car they drive, the quality of the clothes they wear, physical appearances, and, yes, even the church they attend. Often without realizing it, we pay special attention to people who are higher than us in rank while snubbing those who are of lower rank.

Sociologists refer to this phenomenon as the dominance hierarchy; in colloquial terms, we would call it being king of the hill. Regardless of its name, the rules are pretty much the same. We work to be at the top with power, influence, and prestige. Once there, the goal is to maintain and defend one's position. (See Philippians 3:4-11; Luke 11:43; 14:7-11.)

The couple to Ben's right introduced themselves as small-business owners in Midway, but *small* was hardly the appropriate word, as Ben soon learned.

The husband leaned forward and said, "You know, folks often ask how my masonry business in Midway became such a success. Well, it all started when I inherited it from my father-in-law. We've grown it to a twenty-million-dollar business, but let me tell you, it's not about the money. We've just been blessed with some incredibly dedicated and skilled folks on our team, and we take pride in delivering top-notch craftsmanship to our clients. It's not just about the numbers. It's about building lasting relationships with our community. I'm just grateful to be part of something that means so much to Midway."

"My father actually helped build First Church of Midway back when he owned the company," the wife shared proudly. In recent years, she and her husband had helped make many improvements to the church's exterior, such as donating the material and labor for the white pillars. They had also done masonry work at Midway State University, the district court building, the mayoral mansion, and even Dr. Philips's dental office.

Meanwhile, Cathy had pulled Jessica into a separate conversation.

"Jessica, these are the ladies I mentioned at work the other day. We are all part of the Midway University Scholarship Foundation." Turning to the ladies, she said, "I've been trying to recruit Jessica to be a part of our foundation. Wouldn't she make a great addition?"

The woman who had earlier been introduced as the university registrar spoke up. "We have this wonderful tradition among our group of ladies where we gather at my house for coffee. We're quite proud of our efforts to raise money for local college scholarships. We've managed to make quite an impact, and we'd love to have your fresh perspective and ideas bolster our cause. It's a remarkable group. You should join us. I'm sure you'll find it both inspiring and fulfilling!"

The invitation and recognition from the older women made Jessica feel accepted, as if she belonged in their group. And like Ben, Jessica felt honored to be accepted by individuals who were successful and socially connected in Midway. She suddenly realized her children had left her side, however, and glanced around to find Noah and Olivia on a long bench playing on Ben's smartphone. Noah met Jessica's gaze with a bored expression, and she smiled and mouthed, "Thank you," to her son.

VOLUNTEERISM

While people volunteer for a variety of motives, sociologists have found that in certain demographic and economic environments—particularly where socioeconomic class differences are subtle—volunteering for the community can help raise a person's status. In other words, volunteering for a project or group can significantly raise a person's social status in a community, above and beyond any existing status already achieved economically. (See Luke 6:32–36.)

As the conversations continued, a man in his mid-fifties approached the group with his wife. Suddenly the conversation came to a screeching halt, and everyone seemed to light up with enthusiasm. All heads turned toward the new couple, the loose circle reforming around the man and woman.

"Well, if it isn't our Mr. Mayor! We haven't seen you around here for months," one of the men said with a jolly and playful expression.

Ben and Jessica felt a bit of whiplash at this point. They had been the center of attention, but as soon as the mayor entered, all eyes were on him. In fact, most of the group had actually turned their backs to Ben and Jessica in order to be part of the mayor's conversation.

Jessica turned to Ben and gave him an awkward look. With no one to talk to, there wasn't much point in staying. To alleviate the awkwardness, Jessica leaned forward and said to Cathy, "We will catch up with you later."

Cathy gave Jessica a warm smile and a nod. However, she quickly turned back to the mayor, as if she didn't want to miss out on any of the conversation. It wasn't necessarily rude, but Jessica couldn't help but sense that the mayor held higher importance for Cathy.

As they left the conversation and walked toward the kids, Ben turned to Jessica. "So, it appears that your boss is pretty tight with the mayor."

Reaching down to take Olivia's hand, Jessica replied, "Yes, I think they are pretty close. Dr. Philips plays golf with Mayor Archer at least once a week."

Ben was no great investigator—he was more of a black-and-white, dollars-and-cents type of guy—but it was fairly obvious to him that Ruth Archer and the Archer Fellowship Hall must have some connection to Mayor Archer. And the fact that the church used the district court building parking lot made more sense now that they knew the state attorney was a member there. His conversation with the masonry family had revealed a network of deep generational ties to the church as well as connections to the university, district court, mayor, and dentist.

The family meandered together through the fellowship hall for a bit. Ben, realizing they were just walking aimlessly, looked at Jessica. "Want to take off?"

Letting out a breath she didn't realize she was holding, Jessica responded, "Yes, I would like that very much."

On the walk back to their SUV, no one talked much. Jessica welcomed the comfort of their familiar car, sighing, and wondered why they all seemed so exhausted. The church service and interactions had been draining for some reason, as if there were some unseen pressure or burden. Everyone had been positive and supportive, so what was the burden they were feeling?

• • • • • • • • • • • • • • • • • • •

Let us examine First Church of Midway according to our two questions of unity and purpose. It could be said that the unity of First Church of Midway centered on social validation (i.e., acceptance). And a main purpose of attending First Church of Midway was to be noticeable (i.e., to be seen supporting the community).

The Campbells picked up on subtle nuances related to social status during their visit to First Church of Midway. They felt unspoken pressure to "keep up with the Joneses" and to fit in. In the church culture at First Church of Midway, everyone was trying to compete with or emulate the lifestyles of those they considered successful. Churches can sometimes become venues for people to receive social validation, which then provides a sense of belonging. Joining—and remaining in—an influential and successful group of people often gives individuals a sense of achieving an elite social or economic standing. Social goals can have a positive effect, as they motivate individuals to strive for success. However, attempting to maintain a certain image or status can often lead to financial stress, lack of contentment, and superficiality.

For example, Ben and Jessica felt a sense of belonging when visiting with Dr. Philips, Cathy, and their circle. They received a warm welcome because of Jessica's connections at the dental practice, but the group was clearly curious as to where they should place this new family in the social hierarchy. Unlike the rest of the circle, the Campbells had average careers, limited involvement in Midway's societal affairs, and no history in Midway. The Campbells' place in the group's eyes became clear when everyone physically turned away from them once the mayor joined the conversation. Instead of introducing the mayor to the Campbells and allowing the mayor and his wife to welcome a new family to the church as fellow Christians, the circle quickly forgot the Campbells. Clearly, the mayor was more socially important to the group of longtime members at that moment.

The group's interactions also made it clear that attendance at First Church of Midway was not the end all be all of social validation for its members. Remember the joking comment made to the mayor about how he had not been attending consistently? The mayor's social validation did not depend on his attendance at First Church of Midway. Rather, the church bolstered the validation its members received in the community. Members also sought out a socioeconomic validation in the wider, nonchurch affairs of Midway. As demonstrated by the mayor, members considered church attendance to be of secondary importance and really only necessary when a person wanted to display their social commitment in the public-spiritual platform known as First Church of Midway.

THE WORLD AS A STAGE

In Matthew 6:1-4, Jesus confronted the problem of doing good to others while making a performance out of it. That is to say, when Christians do good for someone else, they do not need to call attention to themselves but rather should do their acts of goodness quietly and unobtrusively. However, too often, people will make a theater out of their good deeds—acting compassionately as long as someone is watching. They do their good works to play to the crowds, hoping to get applause and accolades. Even though the works are good and the world may be applauding, the Lord does not think of appearances,

> choosing the lowly things among us to demonstrate His glory rather than applauding our feeble attempts to create glory for ourselves. (See 1 Corinthians 1:27.)

What was the primary purpose of First Church of Midway? Consider all the small things that the visiting Campbell family noticed: the stamp on the inside of the hymnal, the giving wall, the name of the fellowship hall, the use of the district court parking lot, the showy masonry work, and so forth. The giving and volunteerism at First Church of Midway were done in notable and memorable ways; members wanted their efforts to be seen and admired as a way to maintain their standing in the church and community. For example, it was easy to spot important names, the who's who of the church. While people often volunteer their time and give of their assets for noble reasons, many of the members of First Church of Midway also gave of their time and talent for the sake of publicity.

Therefore, the main purpose of First Church of Midway was different from The Quest's mission to provide the best customer experience, Parkside Community Fellowship's desire to create a safe haven from the world, and Mercy Hill Church's passion for providing mercy. First Church of Midway emphasized notoriety in Midway; its purpose was to provide a platform for members to show their commitment to the community. Their mission statement could be stated as "Members who give care; members who care give." Indeed, First Church of Midway was a venue for members to volunteer and give for the sake of being noticed.

KINGDOM OF HEAVEN

In the kingdom of heaven, there is no such thing as a high school popularity scale. There is no such thing as a dominance hierarchy in Christ's church. There is no social totem pole.

These kinds of systems do not exist in the church. Acceptance in Christ's church does not look to a person's accomplishments, spiritual résumé, popularity, status, degrees earned, or offering amount. Furthermore, the good works Christians do should be for the sake of their neighbor, not for themselves, and not for the advancement of a socioeconomic status. Worldly status markers mean nothing in the kingdom of God and contribute nothing to justification. (See Galatians 3:28.)

- -

As the Campbells drove back over the bridge and through the old downtown, they continued to be a bit subdued. Their experience at First Church of Midway had visibly unsettled them.

Breaking the silence, Jessica finally said, "You know, I love my job. Dr. Philips is great to work for, and Cathy has been so nice to me. But I don't want to go back to that church."

Ben nodded his head. "I agree, Jess. I have enough pressure at work already. I don't want to have it on Sundays."

Olivia and Noah overheard their parents' comments, but this time they had no objections. Olivia had had a favorable opinion of Mercy Hill, and Noah had wanted to play dodgeball at Parkside Community Fellowship, but the kids didn't seem concerned at all about not returning to First Church of Midway. They had hardly even been noticed, let alone made to feel accepted.

Noah spoke up from the backseat. "Um, Mom, Dad? It felt like something was missing at that church today. I don't want to go back either."

Chapter 4 Study Guide

REVIEW

1. What unites the members of First Church of Midway?
2. What is the purpose of First Church of Midway?
3. How did the architecture, floor plans, furnishings, sights, and sounds convey the unity and purpose of First Church of Midway?

DISCUSS

1. Think of a time when you did not feel accepted. What was it about the social setting that caused you to notice you did not fit in?
2. Does the biblical church take a person's worldly status or abilities into consideration when it comes to the doctrine of justification?
3. If good works are good, why is it problematic in the church to do them for all to see?
4. Why was it not important for the mayor to be at church consistently?

REFLECT

1. Noah said, "It felt like something was missing at that church today. I don't want to go back." What was missing from First Church of Midway?

Cornerstone Community Church

Despite their unsettling visit to First Church of Midway, Ben and Jessica agreed that they should not give up so easily on finding a church. They decided to take the rest of the summer to keep searching for a church to call home before giving up. And so, this week, they found themselves heading southwest of their house to Cornerstone Community Church.

Ben had overheard coworkers mention how laid-back and friendly it was. After feeling out of place at First Church of Midway, he thought Cornerstone sounded like a safe bet. His coworkers hadn't invited him, but he had been impressed with how much they seemed to enjoy their church when they would talk about the sermons in the break room on Monday mornings.

As they were driving to Cornerstone, they approached a green traffic sign that said "Clayton: Population 17,000."

"What's Clayton?" Noah asked.

"It's the city next to Midway," Jessica replied. "We just left Midway and are now in Clayton."

As the Campbells pulled up to Cornerstone Community Church, it immediately reminded them of The Quest. Many commercial and department buildings surrounded the church.

However, unlike The Quest, Cornerstone Community Church stood on its own and had clearly been built as a church.

After parking the SUV, the Campbells walked toward the building, unsure of where to enter. Ben looked around and eventually spotted a sign that stated "Cornerstone Community Church: Clayton Campus." Underneath the main heading, arrows pointed left for the "Administration Building," straight ahead for the "Resource Center," and to the right for "Main Entrance: Auditorium." Ben started to tell Jessica, but she was already guiding Noah and Olivia to the right, having seen the sign herself.

Inside, the church continued to remind them of The Quest. Coffee was available in the entryway; however, it was self-service. Clear signage in the entryway indicated that Olivia could join others her age for a "fun, safe, and kid-friendly service to help develop world changers." After a bit of conversation, Ben and Jessica decided to take both Olivia and Noah into the auditorium with them.

In the auditorium, the Campbells found four padded seats (though, to Ben's slight disappointment, they did not recline) from which they could easily see the single large screen set into the wall behind the stage. Ben looked around the space as Jessica helped Olivia get situated. Compared to The Quest, the auditorium had a more permanent feeling, as the duct system on the ceiling was not exposed. The stage area held a table with a small cross, a glass podium in front of the table, and musical instruments to the right.

Soon the service started. After the announcements, songs from the band, and Scripture readings, a well-groomed man came to the podium. He wore a collared dress shirt, slacks, and a large silver wristwatch that reflected the light shining on the podium. Glancing at the bulletin, Ben read that this was "Pastor Jonathan."

"Good morning. Today we are going to continue our series 'Overcoming Life's Challenges,'" Pastor Jonathan said.

Sudden motion and rustling startled Jessica a bit. Almost everyone in the room had started reaching for pens and pulling out paper. As she looked around, she saw that people had turned the bulletin over to the back side, which held sermon notes and space to write. Printed at the top of the back page was "Overcoming Life's Challenges (Part 3): A series that delves into strategies for overcoming adversity, facing life's challenges with faith and resilience, and finding strength in difficult times."

Pastor Jonathan continued, "Life is unpredictable. It often takes us down unexpected paths, presenting us with challenges that seem insurmountable. Whether it's health issues, financial struggles, broken relationships, or the crushing disappointment of unfulfilled dreams, we all know what it's like to face adversity. We may be tempted to ask, 'Why is this happening to me?' In times like these, we need to remember that trials are a part of the human experience. Today, we must learn the secret of resiliency."

SECRET KNOWLEDGE

In ancient church history, there was a religious and philosophical movement called *Gnosticism* (the *g* is silent). Gnosticism is old and complex, and parts of it still permeate the religious landscape today. One particular emphasis of Gnosticism was to attain "secret knowledge." It promoted the idea that salvation or enlightenment was only for those who possessed secret knowledge. But who had such secret knowledge? It was typically the religious leader. This is completely contrary to Christianity, as there is nothing secret or exclusive about the Gospel: "Christ was publicly portrayed as crucified" (Galatians 3:1), and forgiveness is freely bestowed to all people and nations (see Matthew 28:18–20).

Partway through the sermon, Ben noticed how incredibly quiet the auditorium was. Some people were leaning forward a bit in their chairs, while others were busy writing notes.

"Resilience is the ability to bounce back from adversity," the pastor went on. "It's not about avoiding challenges but about developing the inner strength to withstand them. Resilience is rooted in the understanding that setbacks are not the end of the road but merely detours on our journey. We can learn from our challenges, grow stronger, and become better equipped to face whatever comes next. Just as a tree's roots dig deeper in response to the wind, we, too, can grow stronger through life's storms."

Even though it was their first time attending Cornerstone Community Church, Ben felt like he should be writing something down as well. However, since the sermon had already begun and since it was so quiet, he decided not to draw attention to himself by asking Jessica if she had a spare pen in her purse.

Instead, Ben followed along with the sermon notes on the bulletin as the pastor expounded on five practical points to build inner resilience: (1) cultivate a positive mindset; (2) set realistic goals and expectations; (3) build a support system; (4) develop resilience skills; and (5) learn from setbacks.

MORALISM

Many theologians have asserted that the default mode of the human heart is the need to be moral. Even in Christianity, there is a belief that the Christian's main goal is to go from evil immorality to good morality. Whether Christian, pagan, or unbeliever, every human has a deep-seated desire to be right and good because the Law of God is written on our hearts, accusing and excusing our thoughts, words, and deeds. (See Romans 2:12–16.) The problem, though, is that a person can obtain a certain degree of good morality and still end up in hell. In other words, morality without Christ is not Christianity. When Christianity is reduced to a set of moral concerns and moral expectations without an emphasis on Christ, it becomes moralism. (See Galatians 5:4.)

Following the sermon, the praise band sang several songs about resilience. A man who introduced himself as the associate pastor then led closing announcements. He thanked Pastor Jonathan for his encouraging words of wisdom and recommended that everyone check out Pastor Jonathan's newest book, *Heartfelt Connections: Navigating Life's Tides with Wise Communication*, which was based on a previous sermon series. Pastor Jonathan would be available for a book signing after the service in the church's Resource Center, where the church would provide donuts and coffee.

Noah and Olivia looked directly at Ben when they heard the word *donuts*. Smiling, he gave an approving head nod.

Jessica leaned over, also smiling, and whispered, "You kids are lucky your dad likes anything that's free."

The four Campbells followed the flow of people out of the auditorium toward the church's Resource Center. Along the way, they stopped to peruse several shelves with books for sale, including some written by the senior pastor. One book was titled *Faith over Fear: Navigating Life's Traffic Jams with Divine GPS*. Another book was titled *Heavenly Hustle: Finding God's Purpose in Your Daily Grind*. Jessica picked up *Holy Hacks: Practical Tips for Living Your Best Faith Life* and glanced over the back cover until she felt Olivia tug on her hand.

"Look, Mommy. I see the pastor signing books. I bet he has the donuts too. Let's go!"

Jessica set the book down and let Olivia lead her toward the Resource Center.

When they entered, the kids made a beeline for the donuts. Unlike in the fellowship areas at some of the other churches they had visited, no one immediately came up to greet Ben and Jessica. Instead, many church members were standing in line to get the pastor's newest book signed. Others seemed to be in deep conversation.

Ben scanned the room and noticed a coworker. "Jess, my coworker Josh is over there. Let's go say hi. Kids, why don't you go grab those donuts you were wanting?"

Ben and Jessica made their way toward Josh, who soon noticed Ben and greeted him with a handshake. He introduced them to the group, and everyone went through the formal introductions. Then the conversation seemed to pick right up where it left off.

"I agree with Pastor Jonathan that we all possess the inner power, but sometimes we should admit our struggles. That, too, can be inspiring," Josh said to the group, looking at Ben and Jessica, attempting to include them in the conversation.

A man standing across from Jonathan replied, "Absolutely, but strength isn't about living in our weakness. It is about bouncing back from hardships."

Some in the group nodded their heads; others seemed to disagree. A woman to Josh's left jumped into the conversation with a bit of intensity: "Gentlemen, you both are wrong. Inner power combined with vulnerability is a commanding recipe for godly resilience. It is not about one or the other. It is about finding an equilibrium that helps us flourish during struggles."

The conversation was cordial, but Ben found himself a bit overwhelmed by the back-and-forth exchange. He could sense the competitive spirit as Josh and the others passionately debated the issues discussed in the pastor's sermon, and he felt a rush of inadequacy, much like how he had felt after visiting First Church of Midway. This time, he felt morally inadequate instead of financially.

Feeling the need to join in but not really having anything to add, Ben simply said, "Pastor's sermon was very interesting."

The group focused on him, and Josh asked, "How do you think you will apply it to your life this week?"

Ben chuckled nervously and said, "Well, I guess I'll put up with you in the office."

Jess laughed along with Ben, but they quickly realized no one else had joined in on the joke.

CHASING EDEN

We do not like the suffering, toil, and limitations of this life under the sun. In other words, we desire to get back to the Garden of Eden. Since most of us cannot afford to continually be on vacation in our paradise of choice, we try to maintain comfortable surroundings, naively imagining that a perfect political, economic, social, moralistic utopia could exist if only everyone would get along. We create an idealized vision of a perfect society in our minds and think that putting certain ideas into practice will result in that utopia. Perhaps we even embrace the idea of revolution because we believe a new Eden will be waiting on the other side of such societal change, accessible to us if only we adjust our practices.

But the literal meaning of *utopia* is "no place." That is, the perfect society we imagine does not exist and cannot be attained by imperfect humans. We always fail. We are stuck with the Adamic curse as long as we live in this life under the sun. This is God's judgment upon the sin of the world, and we all experience sin's daily effects. (See Genesis 3.) Only when Christ returns will humans experience again the perfection of Eden and the utopia we so crave.

After the awkward pause, Ben gave Josh a friendly pat on the back and said, "See you at the office tomorrow, man."

Then the Campbells excused themselves and headed back toward the main entrance. As they were walking, a man came up to them and held out a brochure.

"We're thrilled that you've visited our church family. I wanted to share an incredible opportunity with you," the man said, clearly passionate about what he was saying. "Our 'Financial Faith Builders: Biblical Wisdom for Financial Freedom' class has helped so many families like yours take control of their finances and achieve true freedom. No pressure, but seriously, it could change your life! We'd love to have you there to learn, grow, and connect with our community. What do you say? Will you give it a shot?"

"This sounds great," Ben replied. "However, I am an accountant, and we have a fairly good handle on our finances."

The man's face fell slightly, taken aback by Ben's response, before he proffered the brochure again and responded in a winsome tone, "But do you have financial freedom?"

"Yes, we do," Ben said curtly, still on edge from his conversation with Josh and the group. "We are very free."

Sensing his frustration, Jessica placed a calming hand on Ben's arm and leaned forward to take the brochure. "We will gladly look into it. Thank you so much!" she said.

Just then, Olivia and Noah reappeared, Olivia smiling and holding a donut and Noah thumbing through a free copy of the pastor's new book.

"Time to go, kids," Jessica said.

• • • • • • • • • • • • • • • • • • •

What was the purpose of Cornerstone Community Church? We could picture it as climbing a ladder of self-improvement, with the eventual goal of achieving the "good life," through which one can avoid, overcome, and endure life's challenges and adversities. This was demonstrated by the pastor's sermon and books, all aimed at self-improvement in order to avoid life's hardships. The members listened attentively to his wisdom, handed down from his higher position on the ladder, taking note of the secrets the pastor shared for how to climb higher. Succinctly stated, the purpose of Cornerstone Community Church was for its members to arrive at a self-improved utopic bliss. Unlike The Quest's lack of direction, Cornerstone Community Church directed its members to climb up a moralistic self-improvement ladder to be free of life's difficulties.

Consider Ben and Jessica's final conversation with the man who invited them to the financial freedom class. The man attempted to situate the Campbells on a rung of the ladder from which they could begin improving their finances. When Ben responded that their family finances were in good order, he unknowingly placed himself at the top of the ladder, thus removing the need for him to attend the financial class to gain their knowledge. The man reacted not by congratulating Ben for his firm grasp of their family finances but instead by moving the marker, asking if he also had "financial freedom." He moved the goal higher to create a sense of urgency for Ben to attend the class.

This type of response—manipulating the end goal—is common in churches like Cornerstone Community. In other words, the purpose of Cornerstone Community Church will not change, but leaders may lower or raise the goal to keep everyone climbing the ladder. Leaders may lower the goal for some people so they can experience success and stay motivated to keep climbing. However, as with Ben's encounter, leaders can also raise the goal to ensure there is always a felt need and so that they can maintain their position at the top of the ladder with power and control. While moving the spiritual marker can work to temporarily maintain control, sustain motivations, and manipulate morale, it can also erode trust and credibility when members become aware of the inconsistency.

ASSURANCE WITH CHANGING CIRCUMSTANCES

In Philippians 4:12, Paul writes, "In any and every circumstance, I have learned the secret of facing plenty and hunger, abundance and need." Paul learned the "secret" of thanksgiving during good and bad circumstances, but he freely shared it. The secret is that Paul's contentment, assurance, and gratitude were not tied to his ever-changing circumstances. Nor were they tied to his feelings or surroundings. Instead, Paul's contentment, assurance, and gratitude were tied to something outside himself: Jesus Christ. Assurance is found not by hitting a constantly changing target but in Christ, who gives us forgiveness, life, and salvation. Our health may fail, our souls may grow weary, our wallets may empty, and pain may set in; however, Christ remains unchanged. He is the strength of our hearts, the lifter of our heads, our refuge in tribulation, and our ever-present rescuer who promises never to abandon us. His goal is that all should be saved from sin and every evil. He never changes, and He claims us as His own, regardless of our ability to climb. (See Psalm 73:26.)

With that purpose in mind, what united the members of Cornerstone Community Church? What kept members coming back? As the conversation between Josh and the group in the Resource Center displayed, the members showed up for the opportunity to show off their spiritual understanding. They competed with the rest of their group to prove that they were climbing the metaphorical ladder of moral self-improvement. Their unity was one of moralistic intragroup competition. Remember, Ben had noticed the competitive spirit in the group conversation. That environment allowed members to flex their spiritual muscles and show off their climbing skills, so to speak. Rather than competing with outside groups, their group was united by their own internal competition.

And so, what kept members coming back to Cornerstone Community Church was the constructive way the members pushed one another to improve their performance. As the pastor handed out tips from on top, members experienced camaraderie and the feeling of upward movement as they applied the techniques and learned from one another how to climb more effectively.

INWARD VERSUS OUTWARD

So many voices in our culture today try to convince us that we are awesome and have power within. Consider some of these common sentiments: *You can do it! You have what it takes within you to reach your potential. You can do anything you set your mind to. Be legendary. Redefine the impossible. Activate the power within you!*

What do these slogans have in common? They point us inward to our own resources and skills. While some jobs in life require good ol' grit and sweat or a certain set of skills, that is not how Christianity works. The nature of the Christian faith is that God has snatched you not only out of the darkness but also away from yourself, placing you outside of yourself so that you do not depend on your own strength, conscience, experience, or works. Rather, you are anchored to Christ and His gifts. (See John 1:29.) You are anchored to the promises of God, which cannot deceive. (See 2 Corinthians 1:20; Hebrews 6:19.)

> We find Christian hope not within ourselves but in and delivered by Christ. (See Galatians 2:19-20.) Christianity is not about you; it is about Christ, who is for you.

• • • • • • • • • • • • • • • • • • •

Later that night, Ben and Jessica were getting ready for bed. As they fluffed their pillows, Jessica turned to Ben. "I think we have it pretty good, don't we? I mean, you are happy with me and the kids, right? There is nothing you are hiding, is there?"

Concerned, Ben replied with love in his voice, "Jess, of course not, sweetheart. Why would I hide anything from you? I am so lucky to have you. And the kids? They are great. What's bringing this on?"

Looking down, Jessica clarified: "I've been thinking all day about Cornerstone Community Church. The sermon, the finance class, the books on the shelf—they're all supposed to help people, and everyone there was really into it."

She paused, and Ben waited patiently while she tried to formulate her thoughts.

Then she continued, "It's like this: if everyone going to Cornerstone is there to get their life fixed, and they have been going there a long time, either they have a lot of problems to work through or that church isn't really working for them, right?"

Ben couldn't help but laugh, even though he knew he shouldn't. Jessica was right, and she had given voice to what he himself had been struggling with at the church. Did not the abundance of improvement courses, improvement books, and improvement sermons essentially show that the people were unable to make the teachings and principles work? Could it be that the whole church was trying to climb a descending escalator—always climbing but never achieving?

Leaning over to kiss Jessica on the head, Ben smiled, "You, my dear, are spot on. That's why I love you so much."

Smiling back, Jessica said, "Well, what can I say? I guess I'm known for asking a lot of questions."

Ben gazed over at his wife. "I'm so glad that's who you are."

"I guess there's always next week," Jess said with a yawn. "We'll keep searching to find the answer to the question of which church we should go to in this new city. I have to admit, though, I'm getting tired of looking."

Ben yawned too. "I know, sweetie, I know. There was just something missing at Cornerstone too."

Chapter 5 Study Guide

REVIEW

1. What unites the members of Cornerstone Community Church?
2. What is the purpose of Cornerstone Community Church?
3. How did the architecture, floor plans, furnishings, sights, and sounds convey the unity and purpose of Cornerstone Community Church?

DISCUSS

1. Can mankind ever arrive at a perfect political, economic, and social utopia? Why or why not?
2. Pastor Jonathan shared five practical tips in his sermon. Where did this pastor point his congregation for answers?
3. How can pastors become spiritual manipulators with the kind of theology present at Cornerstone Community Church?
4. Why did Ben become agitated by the man who invited them to be a part of the church activities?

REFLECT

1. Do you agree with Jessica's final observations about Cornerstone's purpose?

Peace Bible Church

"So what is the name of the church for today?" Jessica yelled from the kitchen while making eggs for the kids.

Ben was zooming from room to room, looking for his watch, which he had taken off the night before to do some landscaping work in the backyard.

"Peace," Ben replied from the living room.

"What?" Jessica said.

"Peace Bible Church," Ben restated.

Piecing a couple of things together in her mind, Jessica looked up at Ben as he entered the kitchen. "Isn't that the church that recently hosted that political conference? How many times have I seen that same billboard?" she sighed.

Ben laughed, realizing that the church and its billboard had reminded Jessica of her ongoing battle with the traffic light at Fourteenth Street. Every time she was running late for work, she seemed to hit that red light. While waiting for what seemed to be an eternity, she had plenty of time to read a billboard advertising the "Fifth Annual Faith Emancipation Conference."

Peace Bible Church held the Faith Emancipation Conference each year around the Fourth of July. The conference was very popular in Midway, even garnering national attention, because the chairman of the church was a state representative. Representative Miller was active at the church when the House was not in session, and through his political connections, the church was able to attract prominent speakers for the conference. The year before, the conference had featured a former prisoner of war who had suffered underneath a ruthless foreign dictatorship. As Jessica had seen on the billboard, this year's conference had hosted a famous retired football player who had become a political podcaster.

When the Campbells pulled up to Peace Bible Church, they noticed a large American flag on one side of the church sign and a state and Christian flag on the other. The sign read, "Peace Bible Church: Serving God, Loving Country, Building Community." The church itself was not particularly old but also did not seem brand new. It had a low roofline except for a modest steeple and only one prominent building structure, so the Campbells had no trouble figuring out which door to enter.

HISTORY OF FLAGS

If you were to consult pictures of American church sanctuaries from the early 1900s, you likely would not find any flags. Churches added flags to their sanctuaries in the 1940s during World War II to display patriotism. Especially in churches with German ethnicities, the flag was a way to show that they were not Nazi sympathizers. And while the familiar blue-and-white Christian flag was created in the late 1800s, it was not adopted by the Federal Council of Churches until 1942. As a result, the Christian flag slowly made its way into church sanctuaries from the 1950s onward.

"Welcome to Peace Bible Church!" one of the greeters said, handing each Campbell a rather thick bulletin before pointing them toward the sanctuary.

As they took their seats, some inserts from Jessica's bulletin slipped out and fell on the floor. Noticing that she was a bit flustered, Ben handed her his own bulletin and quickly bent down to pick up half a dozen inserts. Several inserts pertained to various activities in the church; however, one insert caught Ben's eye. It was a glossy half-sheet titled "Voter's Guide." On the front, it had a picture of Representative Miller and his upcoming opponent, Mrs. Emily Johnson. Below each of their pictures was a list of their political stances on issues such as abortion rights, climate change policies, immigration, gun control, healthcare, and criminal justice reform. On the back, there was a similar chart for the upcoming governor and presidential races.

Ben reorganized the inserts and sat down next to Jessica, who had also been reading the voter's guide. From her facial expression, she was deep in thought, so Ben began to read another insert.

This one showcased the events of the recent Faith Emancipation Conference and provided information on how members could obtain audio or video recordings of the conference. A picture of the NFL cornerback turned political podcaster who had spoken at the conference caught his eye. Ben had never listened to the podcast, but he wondered whether the man's perspective aligned with what he knew about Peace Bible Church's policies and values. Ben wasn't sure how he felt about the unexpected detour into the political arena, even if he agreed with the conference's stances. He wondered how tightly these worlds of faith and politics were intertwined at Peace Bible Church. Ben couldn't help but wonder whether he wanted to be reminded of politics every Sunday.

TWO CITIZENSHIPS?

If you were born in the United States, you have a birth certificate showing that you were born in a particular state at a particular time in a particular county. The birth certificate testifies that you are a citizen of the United States of America by birth. Christians also have a baptismal certificate. Our baptismal certificate is a testimony that we are citizens of God's kingdom. At your Baptism, Christ claimed you as His own. The Lord delivered you from the dominion of sin, death, and the devil; He rescued you from a citizenship of demise and made you a citizen of the kingdom of heaven. (See Philippians 3:20-21.) Therefore, because you were physically born of a woman and spiritually born again at the baptismal font—because you have these two certificates—you are citizens of two kingdoms, two realms, at the same time. (See Romans 13:1-7.)

"Good morning."

At the voice, the Campbells looked up and directed their attention to the front of the church.

"It is good to be with God's people," the man said.

Ben looked back down at his bulletin, wondering if this man was the pastor and whether his name was listed, but he didn't find anything.

The man highlighted several activities in the church. After a brief pause, he said, "I want to draw your attention to Thursday here at the church. This Thursday evening at seven, we have an important church event. We have our local caucus meeting over in the fellowship hall to discuss issues close to our hearts. Let's be active citizens and let our faith at Peace Bible Church guide our political involvement. I hope to see you all there."

Then the service started. One of the musicians asked the congregation to pull out a thin white book from the pews, which held easy-to-follow choruses for them to sing. Members of the church also came forward to share several Scripture readings and short prayers. After the last prayer, a man stepped into a raised

CHAPTER 6 | PEACE BIBLE CHURCH

pulpit. Ben realized then that this man must be the pastor, and the man making the announcements must have been another member of the church.

"Fellow Christians, today I want to talk to you about the values that we hold dear and how they are essential in today's difficult culture," the pastor stated with conviction. "The foundation of our nation is built on these values. Our nation echoes the very essence of our faith. As you know, there are forces in our world that are advocating for evil. They are attempting to do away with the importance of the family. And so, it is of utmost importance that we, as Christians of Peace Bible Church, let our faith guide our political decisions this fall as we cast our votes in the ballot box."

The sermon continued for quite some time as the pastor elaborated on Scripture, the Constitution, and the cultural history of the United States. Ben had the same political affiliation as the pastor, so he did not feel out of place, but he was still a bit confused by the amount of political content in the sermon. The few times he glanced over at Jessica, she, too, seemed confused and thoughtful, wearing the same expression she'd had when reading the voter's guide earlier.

The pastor eventually concluded the sermon with an emotional command. "You, as a church, have the power to lead our great nation forward to a brighter future that is in harmony with our deeply held beliefs."

WHAT NOT TO EXPECT IN A SERMON

While a sermon may be entertaining, it should not be exclusively about entertainment. We can find entertainment anywhere—on our phones, at the movies, in a book. Instead, a sermon must tell listeners something they can't hear at the movies or while playing on their phones.

A sermon can give practical advice, but it also needs to tell listeners something they can't learn in a self-help book or life-hack video.

And while it is not inappropriate for a sermon to address social and political difficulties in culture, it should do so only when the biblical text refers to political ideas. Nor should a sermon be a repeat broadcast of the nightly news, focusing on the talking points of a political party or of like-minded constituents. (See Acts 17:16–31.)

After the service, Ben and Jessica were gathering their things, and the man who made the announcements approached them. "Good morning. It is always nice to see new faces here at Peace Bible Church. My name is Richard."

Ben and Jessica each shook his hand and explained that they were new to Midway. As the conversation continued, Jessica shared how much they loved their new house and what part of Midway it was in.

Clearly excited, Richard exclaimed, "Well, isn't that something! I'm your representative."

At Jessica's confused look, he explained, "I am the state representative for District 3, which includes that part of Midway. I represent you in the State House!"

Seeing that Jessica now understood, Richard—Representative Miller—leaned forward. "Have you ever been to a caucus meeting?"

"No, we haven't," Jessica replied.

"Well, let me tell you," Richard continued without hesitation, "these meetings are a fantastic way to get involved and have your voices heard. It's like a big neighborhood chat with people who care about the same issues as you."

Jessica appreciated the invitation, but she was starting to feel overwhelmed by Representative Miller's enthusiasm.

Seeing her body language, Representative Miller lowered his intensity a bit. "These caucus meetings are not all politics. It's about making a difference in your community. Plus, we've got some great guest speakers lined up. You'll be amazed at how inspiring they can be. I heard there might even be some homemade apple pie this time," he said with a wink. "Think about it. You will be glad you came. I promise."

Ben, also noticing Jessica's discomfort, was about to step in when he felt Olivia, who had been very subdued all morning, tug at his shirt.

"Can we go home, Daddy?" she whispered.

Ben tousled her hair and whispered back, "You bet, kiddo."

Overhearing them, Noah let out a big sigh and said, "Finally!"

Ben quickly said their goodbyes and led the family through the poster-filled front doors to their SUV.

GIVE UNTO CAESAR AND UNTO GOD

Christians are not secularists living only and exclusively by the authority of the state. Christians are also not monks living only and exclusively by the authority of the church. Christians are citizens of both the state and the kingdom of God, which means that Christians give unto Caesar what belongs to Caesar and unto God what belongs to God. (See Matthew 22:21.) If the church gets greedy, taking what belongs to Caesar, the Christian shall then resist the church's overreach with calm resolve. And if the state gets greedy and takes what belongs to God (see Daniel 6:1-23)? The Christian shall then resist with calm resolve as well. The Christian cannot give to the state the authority that belongs to the realm of the church or vice versa.

• • • • • • • • • • • • • • • • • • • •

Let us consider Peace Bible Church according to our main questions: What was its purpose? What united the members?

The interactions the Campbells had clearly showed that Peace Bible Church's purpose was to advance specific political policies. Though the sermons, activities of the church, and conversations of the members sounded Christian and morally upright, they ultimately promoted certain government policies, legislation, and voting. The church functioned much like a Christianized political party, think-tank, or action committee. All ideological roads in Peace Bible Church led to the state capitol.

This brings us back to our earlier discussion of the three estates: the church, the state, and the family. Like Mercy Hill Church, Peace Bible Church overstepped into the other estates. The most obvious example is how they overstepped into the realm of the state, as seen by the emphasis on political causes in the sermon and the Campbells' reactions to it. However, Peace Bible Church also crossed into the estate of the family by attempting to politically coerce the family's decision-making process.

Like every Christian, the Campbells are citizens of both the church and state. They are called to walk in the laws of the land. They are to pay their taxes, vote, serve and be active in their communities, follow speed limits, follow state laws, and possibly take up arms to support and defend the nation. The Campbells are simultaneously called to abide in the church. They are to regularly hear the Word of God and receive the Lord's gifts in the church, as well as to worship, praise, and give thanks. And so, the Campbell family is called to participate in the estates of the state and church.

DISOBEYING, BEARING WITNESS, AND CHANGING POLICY

When the state acts badly, Christians can attempt to enact change by voting for different candidates, disapproving ballot measures, and so forth. When the state compels Christians to act immorally, the Christian must peacefully disobey. (See Acts 5:29.) And finally, when the government permits activities contrary to God's Law, the Christian bears witness by not conforming to the government's laws but living and confessing as God intends.

However, just because the Campbells abide both in the church and in the state does not mean that the church itself should abide in the realm of the state. In other words, Peace Bible Church is not a person. Nor is Peace Bible Church a political action group working to influence the state. Peace Bible Church is a church, an estate distinguished from family and state. The ministry of the Word and Sacraments belongs to the estate of the church, and political causes belong to the estate of the state. The church functions independently and separately from the state, not under, for, or within the state. By focusing only on advancing certain political causes, Peace Bible Church found their purpose in the realm of the state instead of the church.

The Campbells' interactions also made clear what united the members of Peace Bible Church: common political association. Members kept coming back to be united with like-minded individuals, share their values, and collectively work toward common goals. Such political associations can often foster a sense of community and belonging, especially when people feel like they have a common enemy to oppose. But the church is more than a place to pursue political causes together.

HOW CHURCHES INFLUENCE POLITICS

Do churches have a role in politics? The answer is yes, but only indirectly. The church shapes Christians by proclaiming God's Word. As they are shaped by the church and God's Word, Christians are then equipped to vote, run for office, enact policy changes, calmly disobey ungodly laws, bear witness when the state fails to enact godly laws, and otherwise influence the world.

And so, we do not need Christian judges, Christian police officers, Christian members of Congress, Christian voters, and so forth, as if the state were a direct extension or arm of the church. And just because a person is a Christian does not automatically qualify him or her to hold a public office, like being a judge, for example. On the other hand, the church and state should not be so divided that we see the state as only secular and the church as only religious. The state does not have the right to be free from the ethics and values of the church, for the state belongs to the Lord just as the church does. (See Romans 13:1–7.) Instead, Christians who are formed and informed by the Word of God should enter into the estate of the government to faithfully execute their duties as judges, police officers, members of Congress, and voters.

. . . .

Later that night, Ben was watching his nightly news program as usual. He furrowed his brow, thinking about their morning.

"Jess, Peace Bible Church this morning was . . . different."

Nodding, Jessica responded, "Yes, it was. I agreed with their political positions, but I feel like that's all they talked about."

"Exactly!" Ben replied. "I find politics fascinating, and don't get me wrong, they are important, but things seemed to be out of place this morning."

After several seconds of quiet, Ben sighed and said, "I am sure they are unaware of how one-sided they are."

"What do you mean?" Jessica asked. Ben was not the type to ride the fence politically speaking, so she was confused by his statement.

"Sorry, I am not saying that they should be balanced politically," Ben quickly clarified. "You know I appreciate people who stick to their guns. I am just saying that it seems that a church should balance the important issues while also not neglecting what the church is supposed to be about." Ben stopped again, thinking over what he had just said. "I don't know if the word *balance* is even right."

Smiling, Jessica walked over to him. "I say we just cross that church off the list. There's still a month left of summer before school starts, so we have time to find our new church family."

Ben stood up and gave her a hug. "I love you, Jess. You are right. We will be fine."

Chapter 6 Study Guide

REVIEW

1. What unites the members of Peace Bible Church?
2. What is the purpose of Peace Bible Church?
3. How did the architecture, floor plans, furnishings, sights, and sounds convey the unity and purpose of Peace Bible Church?

DISCUSS

1. How would you respond if your pastor announced a political sentiment with which you adamantly disagreed?
2. Is it fair to say that just as Mercy Hill Church overstepped into the estate of the family, Peace Bible Church is overstepping into the estate of the government?
3. Is there a time and place when a church and Christians should disobey and speak against the government?
4. What is the difference between a Christian judge and a judge who is Christian? Why is this subtle distinction important to understand?

REFLECT

1. Ben said, "It seems that a church should balance the important issues while also not neglecting what the church is supposed to be about." What should Peace Bible Church be about?

AUGUST 6

Trinity Church

The Campbells had traveled back to Fairview to see family and old friends over the previous weekend. As much as they had wanted to attend church with family, the whole group had decided at the last minute to crash overnight at a friend's cabin in the foothills west of Fairview. Long story short, they woke up late on Sunday morning with a dead battery and no jumper cables. Needless to say, it was a fun but exhausting weekend for the Campbells.

Everyone hit the ground running on Monday morning after their return, which meant the following Saturday was a full day of recovery.

Opening the microwave to grab her mug of hot water, Jessica bantered, "So, hubby, what adventure awaits us tomorrow morning?"

Smiling, Ben replied, "I heard from a client this week about Trinity Church down on Thirty-Second Street."

Jessica placed a bag of decaf Earl Grey in her mug for her typical evening tea and said, "I wonder if it's near that boutique I like. What time is the service?"

Ben thought for a moment. "Yes, I think it is close to the boutique. And the service starts at ten. Apparently this church has a lot of historic roots here in Midway, and it runs a two-year Bible college."

"Sounds interesting. Maybe we can stop at the boutique afterward!" Jessica remarked with a grin.

The next morning, the Campbells headed ten minutes southwest of their house to Trinity Church. The church was in a residential area with a lot of older but well-maintained homes, perhaps from the early 1900s. Large, old trees lined the streets. Olivia poked her head out the window as they drove, admiring the canopy of leafy branches overhead. This area of Midway felt very established and historical. It was also neat and clean.

The sky opened up a bit as they neared the church and its large parking lot on the east side of the road. The all-brick exterior and modest steeple of Trinity Church matched the stately, historic feel of the surrounding neighborhood. Unlike Parkside Community Fellowship and some of the other churches the Campbells had visited, Trinity Church seemed to be one large structural unit, with no visible building additions.

WHAT IS A DENOMINATION?

A denomination is a group of churches and Christians who share common beliefs, practices, and traditions. They often have their own hierarchical order, joint rituals, and a particular set of local and worldwide goals.

A sign with a large digital screen flashed various announcements as Ben turned into the parking lot.

"That must be their logo," Jessica commented as the screen flashed to a new slide, causing the rest of the family to take notice as well.

The symbol on the screen matched the permanent emblem on the base of the sign. The emblem featured an elegant gold cross at its center with a small Bible and a dove on either side, all encircled by a blue border. The church's name and denomination were listed in gold script below the border. Though the logo was not unappealing, the font selection and clip art aesthetic dated it a bit.

As the Campbells approached the church, they saw the same blue-and-gold logo above the main doors. A couple in their early sixties greeted the family when they walked in. As the man handed Ben a bulletin, Ben noticed a pin on the lapel of the man's jacket. It was the same blue-and-gold logo! After seeing the logo on the greeter, Ben chuckled to himself. The game was on. How many more blue-and-gold logos could he find? He started glancing around the foyer.

Before the Campbells could walk much farther, another older gentleman approached them and reached out his hand. "Morning! Welcome to Trinity. I'm Jim."

Ben shook his hand. "Ben Campbell, and this is my wife, Jessica, and our kids, Noah and Olivia."

Jim raised his finger to his chin. "Campbell? I knew some Campbells once upon a time in New Rockford. Yes, Tom and Susan Campbell. Any relationship to you?"

Thinking quickly through his dad's family tree, Ben answered, "I don't think so. My family roots don't extend that far east."

Nodding his head, Jim responded, "Shucks, it is always fun to make connections. I used to serve at New Hope Church in New Rockford. The Campbells were a great family. So supportive of the church, especially our Building Bridges program and the Holtz missionary family."

The conversation continued for a bit, and Jim welcomed them again to Trinity Church.

DENOMINATIONAL NEPOTISM

Nepotism is when people are given preferential treatment on the basis of their family ties or last names instead of their qualifications, skills, or abilities. Denominational nepotism, then, is when someone is accepted or overly favored in a church not on the basis of Christ or their baptismal identity but on the basis of their connections to influential people in a church's heritage or denominational hierarchy.

The old saying "blood is thicker than water" is often used to convey the idea that family relationships are stronger than casual connections. However, for the church, water is thicker than blood—meaning that one's baptismal identity supersedes any nepotistic bond. (See Matthew 3:9-10; John 8:39-40.)

Ben grinned when they entered the sanctuary. Extending from the back wall, front and center, was the blue-and-gold church logo, lit by blue lights.

"Five," he murmured.

"Five what?" Jessica asked, confused.

Ben laughed. "Sorry, I didn't realize I said that out loud. That makes five times I have seen the blue-and-gold logo. Twice it was on the sign, then it was on the building, then it was on the greeter's lapel, and now it's here in the sanctuary."

Jessica chuckled and shook her head in disbelief at Ben's little game. "Five? Really?"

Without hesitation, Ben held up the bulletin and pointed to the front page. "Nope, six!"

INSIDE BASEBALL

The phrase "inside baseball" is used to describe conversations and discussions that require behind-the-scenes or specific knowledge about a particular topic or circumstance. The term is often used when people are discussing details or intricacies that are not widely known to outsiders or the general public.

At ten on the dot, a younger man in a white robe came to the front of the sanctuary and welcomed everyone to Trinity Church.

"Good morning, everyone! As you know, Pastor Anderson is out of town this weekend again for meetings at the denominational headquarters. He won't be back until late in the week. Our prayers go forth for him and the board as they make some important decisions regarding the Building Bridges program as well as the Renewal Ministries Initiative. Also, today we want to recognize Dr. and Mrs. Davis, who are here with us for the week teaching at the Bible college. Dr. Davis, we are so proud of the work you have done overseas with Pathways of Hope in Ghana."

Dr. Davis stood up and gently waved at everyone in the pews.

The younger man continued. "If you want to sit in one of the classes with Dr. Davis, please talk to Dr. Philips, and he will fit you into one of the classes at the Bible college. Finally, I want to mention that we are taking a special offering today for the Building Bridges program and the Renewal Ministries Initiative. Both of these programs are important for our denomination and its future. So please make sure to be involved in using your gifts to support these two programs. There will be two special plates in the back to collect your gifts today and next Sunday. Please know that your gifts for these two important programs will be listed on this year's giving record for your tax purposes."

After the announcements, the service continued with several modern-sounding hymns, a Scripture reading, an engaging sermon about Christian loyalty, and several prayers for the local church and the ministry goals of the denomination.

PHILANTHROPIC RIVALRY

Many people give of their resources to make a positive impact on society or within an organization. However, some people and organizations engage in philanthropy not for godly reasons but out of a desire to enhance their public image. In some cases, individuals and organizations can even become competitive as they try to outdo one another in giving. The amount of giving becomes a virtue signal of who is ultimately supreme. It becomes a way to self-justify. (See Matthew 23:23; Luke 18:9–14.)

When the service ended, most people filed out to the narthex and began mingling.

"Should we take a look around the building a bit?" Jessica asked, eyeing the crowd.

"Yeah, let's go explore," Olivia said. "Maybe this church will have donuts somewhere too."

They turned left after exiting the sanctuary, which led them down a hallway filled with portraits. Ben and Jessica walked over and saw that they were pictures of the former presidents of the church denomination. As they moved down the hall, the dates on the bottom of the pictures got older and older. Olivia and Noah, clearly less interested in the history, kept going down the hallways.

Suddenly, Olivia pointed and said, "Mom and Dad, look, *Campbell!* This guy has the name Campbell."

Walking over to the picture, Ben and Jessica read the inscription: "William Campbell, 1928–1943."

"That was President Campbell. He served us well during World War II," a voice said behind the Campbells.

Ben and Jessica both jumped a bit, startled, before turning around hesitantly. The man had a warm expression, which put them more at ease.

"Good morning. My name is Ronald Young," the man said kindly.

After the Campbells introduced themselves, Ronald pointed over at the painting. "So, any relationship to President Campbell?" he asked.

Ben and Jessica shook their heads, and Ben repeated the explanation he had given to Jim earlier. As they chatted, Ben noticed the same pin on Ronald's lapel. He couldn't help himself, so he gestured at it and said, "I'm sorry, I don't mean to be rude, but I have seen that logo everywhere this morning. Your pin is the seventh time I've seen it. What exactly is it?"

"It is our denominational seal and the logo of our church," Ronald answered, his voice expressing deep sentiment. He led them over to another portrait on the wall, and Ben and Jessica were surprised to see that the portrait was of him.

"I was the president of our denomination for eighteen years and a pastor before that. I moved to Midway after my wife passed away two years ago. We have quite a few retired pastors in this church, as well as professors from the Bible college. We are good old friends who go way back. Plus, it helps to have a lot of great people to keep this church in line with national leadership."

The Campbells could tell that the memories were fond for Ronald, who continued sharing about his experience at Trinity Church.

"It is so good to be in this congregation. Pastor Anderson and the members here have such a devotion to our denomination. Pastor Anderson is phenomenal, and he is so instrumental at our headquarters. I am not quite sure how many projects he is involved with there, but I do know he does a great job balancing the parish and his leadership responsibilities. He seems to be gone every other week."

Ben and Jessica smiled but couldn't contribute much, as they had never met Pastor Anderson and didn't really know anything about the denomination or its history.

Ronald noticed that he was starting to dominate the conversation, so he quickly concluded, saying, "Even though Trinity is not the biggest congregation in our denomination, it is one of the biggest contributors of finances and talent, that is for sure."

AUTHORITATIVE SOURCES FOR THEOLOGY

Every church has an authoritative source for its theology. That is to say, each church derives its theology, guidance, and discernment from somewhere, whether that source is tradition, its members, denominational leadership, a so-called direct revelation from the Holy Spirit, the ancient church, local cultural norms, the Bible, and so forth. But what happens when conflicts arise or the church has questions about its theology? Where will the church turn for an authoritative word for correction, rebuke, and guidance? Will the church turn to the Bible as the final authoritative guide for faith and conduct, or will it instead prioritize local customs, the opinions of its members, or the policies of denominational leadership? (See 2 Timothy 3:16.)

• • • • • • • • • • • • • • • • • • •

Let's take a step back and examine the Campbell family's experience at Trinity Church. Several nuances will help us determine the church's unity and purpose.

One of the first things the Campbells noticed was the prominent logo. From the main sign to the sanctuary to the members' attire, the church highlighted the denominational logo as its identifying marker, showing its importance to the members of Trinity.

Denominational ties also played a big role in the interactions Ben and Jessica had with the members. The announcements before the service all centered on denominational initiatives and pointing out big names in the denomination, assuming everyone would have knowledge of their church culture. And though the people Ben and Jessica met were kind, their conversations, too, were focused on denominational connections. Both Jim and Ronald attempted to connect the Campbells to well-established people from the church.

HERITAGE, TRADITIONS, AND POLICIES

Every group has its own heritage, traditions, and policies, including churches. However, churches must carefully examine their traditions to make sure they serve to teach parishioners and elevate the message of Christ. If they do, then these good faith traditions and ceremonies can be preserved. But any tradition developed from our own self-centered opinions, desires, and agendas that opposes Christ and His gifts must be rejected. (See Mark 7:1-13.) The same goes for policies and church governance. A policy or church governance is only good if it serves the end goal of teaching people what they need to know about Christ. (See Luke 4:16-30.)

Likewise, the presidential hallway communicated to the Campbells that Trinity Church highly valued their denomination's history and culture. Perhaps Ronald's comment conveyed it best: "It helps to have a lot of great people to keep this church in line with national leadership." Clearly, the authoritative source for Trinity Church was the denomination.

And so, what united Trinity Church? What was at the center of the church, gave members meaning, and kept people coming back? Where did people feel included and accepted? The answer is denominational heritage. Trinity's unity was in the heritage, programs, and ethos of the denomination.

But what about Trinity Church's purpose? Consider where the congregation focused its time and money. As the Campbells witnessed, the congregation focused mostly on denominational efforts, and a great deal of special offering money flowed from Trinity to fund those denominational programs. While giving money to a denomination is not bad, members clearly took immense pride in their giving, as Ronald's comments showed, which was problematic.

Members also took pride in the fact that Pastor Anderson spent a lot of his time focused on the national headquarters. Even though they did not completely understand his involvement there, the members of Trinity nonetheless viewed his absences as a good thing because he was serving the denomination. Both the pastor and his flock were focused on advancing the denomination instead of their local congregation. Thus, the purpose of Trinity Church was to support the mission of the larger organizational structure.

THE DOWNWARD TRAJECTORY

The pastoral trajectory is always downward toward the pastor's parishioners—his sheep. While pastors may be called to serve on national boards, denominational task forces, and local committees, they must guard themselves from inadvertently neglecting their sheep. The temptation exists for a pastor to desire upward mobility, longing for accolades and promotions at higher positions of authority in the church. However, a pastor is a true servant only when he, at the bottom with his sheep, has nothing to give except Christ's Word and Sacraments. Likewise, those who serve in higher positions of authority or on boards, task forces, and committees do so in support of local churches, pastors, and church workers as they serve their sheep. The trajectory of a denomination and its church workers must always be downward to suffer for the sheep, not upward toward perceived glory. (See Ezekiel 34:11–16; John 10:11–18; Mark 10:45.)

• • • • • • • • • • • • • • • • • • • •

As the Campbells drove home, Jessica poked Ben and said, "I wonder how much leverage we would have at that church if you were *Doctor* Campbell."

Laughing out loud, Ben said, "You know, I thought about lying for a brief moment, saying that we were indeed related to President William Campbell."

Jessica's jaw dropped. "Benjamin! I would have been mortified if you had done that!"

They all laughed for a bit.

Then Ben said, "In all seriousness, I kind of respect their heritage. They seem to be a close-knit church. They also seem to cherish their history and have an idea of where they need to go."

"I agree," Jessica said thoughtfully, "but how would we even get plugged into that church? I felt like I was on the outside looking in. Would they ever accept us?"

Noah interrupted, "Maybe we should call Grandpa and double-check to see if we are related."

"Or *you* could just become the next president, Daddy!" Olivia chimed in.

Jess smiled back at her kids. "Very creative ideas, you two. But I think something is still missing if we feel like we need to do ancestry research or run for a position to belong."

Chapter 7 Study Guide

REVIEW

1. What unites the members of Trinity Church?
2. What is the purpose of Trinity Church?
3. How did the architecture, floor plans, furnishings, sights, and sounds convey the unity and purpose of Trinity Church?

DISCUSS

1. How are denominations beneficial for members and for those trying to find a church home?
2. Some churches avoid denominations and call themselves nondenominational. Why do you think they want that distinctive label?
3. What did Noah offer as a suggestion to his parents for how to belong to the new church? Do you think if the Campbells had been related, it would have changed how they felt about Trinity Church?
4. This chapter briefly mentioned that the sermon of the day was about loyalty. To whom do we owe our loyalty as Christians?

REFLECT

1. Jessica said, "I think something is still missing if we feel like we need to do ancestry research or run for a position to belong." What was missing from Trinity Church?

Immanuel Church

"Today I had the sweetest gentleman in for a cleaning," Jessica remarked.

Ben looked up from what he was doing, prepared to listen as she shared about her day.

"He was an older man named Jerry, and we had such a wonderful conversation. I got to meet his wife, Helen, too, when I took him out to the waiting room. He's been at the office a lot trying to deal with some dental issues."

Her face fell a bit as she explained that Jerry had fought in Vietnam and hadn't had access to dental care during the war, which led to some long-term dental problems.

"Anyway," she continued, perking back up a bit, "I told him that we were new to Midway, and he invited us to his little church this Sunday."

Ben replied, "That is super, sweetie. What's the church?"

"It's called Immanuel, but here is the thing. It is a country church about thirty-five miles north of downtown."

Thinking through the geography of the area, Ben asked, "So it's in Riverside?"

"No, when I say 'country church,' I mean Jerry and Helen live out of town," Jessica clarified. "Jerry told me that he and his

113

wife used to have a dairy farm after the war, and the church is near his old farm. The way he described it made it sound like the church is in the middle of a field."

Three days later, the Campbells set out for Immanuel Church. Since the church was located north of Midway, the bypass was the quickest way to get there. Some road construction forced them to go south a bit first, taking them right through the Parkside planned community. After several minutes, they turned westward to connect with the bypass, driving past a familiar sign indicating Clayton was a quarter of a mile ahead. They turned onto the bypass and drove north for several miles until the road angled east and took them past the old and new downtowns. After several more minutes of driving, the bypass turned into Highway 5.

"It is a funny feeling passing by all these other churches. We sure have visited a lot of them," Jessica commented.

Ben nodded his head in agreement. "How many more miles until this church?" he asked.

Reaching into her purse, Jessica took out a crumpled piece of paper.

"What's that?" Ben inquired.

With a small laugh, Jessica answered, "Oh, Jerry told me that the church probably isn't on GPS or any online maps. He drew out directions for me on the back of an old grocery list he had in his pocket. Apparently his wife has pretty bad arthritis, so he had been doing the errands lately."

Jessica examined the yellow paper for a second. Then she said, "According to Jerry's sheet, we need to drive north on Highway 5 for another thirty miles. He said to watch for a truck stop named Tom's Truck Haven."

"What a great name—Tom's Truck Haven!" Ben said with a laugh.

"After the truck stop, he said we need to go another mile and turn left by an old abandoned grain elevator, and then travel another four miles on a gravel road," Jessica said, reading again off the paper.

They drove for a while in silence, admiring the scenery as they got farther from the city of Midway.

"Daddy, are we there yet?" Olivia spoke up.

"No, sweetie," Ben replied. "We are on an adventure to find the country church in the middle of nowhere! Look out for Tom's Truck Haven."

Olivia settled back and looked out her window. "I'm a good finder. I'll find it, Daddy."

Sure enough, Olivia was the first to spot the truck stop, and Ben began to follow the rest of Jerry's detailed directions.

After another few minutes, Olivia pointed out the window again. "Is that the church?"

A white church had appeared just ahead, its steeple rising above the surrounding trees. Off to the one side of the church was also a small lake. As the Campbells pulled into the gravel parking lot, they saw an older sign that said "Immanuel Church: Rev. Theodore Reynolds." The sign needed some TLC. The paint was flaking in some spots, and the wood needed fresh stain. There were only twenty or so cars in the parking lot, so the Campbells easily found a spot.

"What are those?" Olivia asked, finding another thing to be curious about.

Looking to the front of the church, Jessica answered, "Oh, those are tombstones, sweetie."

Weathered tombstones surrounded Immanuel Church. The sight was very different from the other churches they had visited. The other churches each had their own curb appeal, but Immanuel Church had an old sign and leaning tombstones, with no professional landscaping, zealous greeters, or preferential parking spots.

As they walked from their SUV to the church, the sidewalk took them through the tombstones. Olivia and Noah were definitely taking it all in.

"Look, Mom, that one has part of my name," Olivia said as they passed one tombstone.

The rest of the family stopped to look at it. Like the others, it was crooked, and it had several lines of text:

OLIVE BENSON
1909–2008
LOVING WIFE, MOTHER, AND GRANDMA
"LAZARUS, COME OUT!"

"Wow," Ben said, "she almost lived to be a hundred years old."

"What does that mean at the bottom, 'Lazarus, come out'?" Noah asked.

Jessica shook her head and responded, "I don't know. I'm not sure why that is printed there."

LAZARUS, COME OUT!

In John 11, we read about a man named Lazarus who died. With many tears, his loved ones wrapped him in burial strips and placed him in a tomb. They said their goodbyes. The pain of death sank into their souls. Jesus approached the tomb of Lazarus, tears running down His own face. And then, with a tear in His eye, Jesus did something amazing—the same thing He will do for all Christians on the Last Day. He shouted, "Lazarus, come out" (v. 43).

Just like that, Lazarus walked out of the tomb, wrapped from head to toe in burial cloths. Jesus told everyone, "Unbind him, and let him go" (v. 44). That day, the Lord called out to Lazarus, and Lazarus was raised from the dead. On the great Last Day, Jesus will call out to the baptized, and they will rise again.

The Campbells made their way into the narthex. Like the outside, the inside of the church had seen better days.

"It smells like Grandpa's shed in here," Olivia whispered to her dad, crinkling her nose a bit.

"That's just how some old buildings are, sweetie," Ben whispered back, noticing an older man walking their way.

"Good morning, Jessica. I am glad you made it. This must be your family," the man said. He extended a hand to Ben and said, "I'm Jerry."

A woman walked over slowly, arriving just as Jerry offered the Campbells some coffee.

"Don't accept the coffee, Jessica!" the woman said immediately. Then she introduced herself to Ben and the kids. "I'm Helen, Jerry's wife, and everyone knows his coffee is bitter and nasty. He insists on buying that cheap coffee from Tom's Truck Haven. Nobody in the county likes it except for Jerry and some of his old vet friends," Helen informed them conspiratorially.

As the conversation continued, Ben and Jessica couldn't help but notice that it felt different from the church meet and greets they had experienced over the past few weeks. Jerry and Helen were friendly and kind, but they didn't mention any church ministries. They weren't looking at their watches to see when church would start, and they did not talk about the pastor. In fact, they didn't mention Immanuel Church or themselves at all. Instead, they asked questions about the Campbells.

THE COMMONPLACE

Most churches have fellowship halls, narthexes, gathering areas, transition spaces, and entrance areas that function as places where common things occur. In these spaces, we can expect everyday things to occur, such as laughing, loud conversations, busyness, eating, drinking coffee, games, jokes, projects, meetings, hanging up coats, and so forth. This is how life operates in the realm of the commonplace.

Jerry and Helen learned about Ben's struggles with his golf slice, Noah's love for soccer, Olivia's plans to start dance lessons in the fall, and even Jessica's favorite boutique on Thirty-Second Street. Partway through the conversation, a bell rang. The Campbells were all caught off guard for a moment.

Helen put a calming hand on Olivia's shoulder and shared, "That is the church bell telling us that service is about to start. Would you and your family be willing to sit next to us?"

Olivia looked up at Jessica as if to get permission.

"We would love that," Jessica responded with a smile.

The Immanuel Church sanctuary was smaller, reminiscent of Mercy Hill Church, except without the many-colored decorations on the altar or either of the two wooden podiums at the front. Instead, each piece was decorated with simple green banners. Unlike the other churches, Immanuel Church had a large cross up front, and it was not empty. In fact, the cross was a crucifix, which portrayed Jesus suffering and dying, as Jerry informed Noah when he asked. The pews were solid oak and had hymnals like First Church of Midway. However, these hymnals were quite shabby. The blue covers were worn, the bookmarks were frayed, and the pages had yellowed.

SACRED PLACES

It is often believed that sacredness is found only in heavenly dimensions, away from the commonness of earth. However, when our Lord comes to interact with mankind, He makes common places sacred. For example, when the Lord distributes His blessed Word and Sacraments in the sanctuary, the sanctuary becomes a sacred place. What makes a sanctuary sacred—indeed, what makes it a sanctuary—is not the decorations or ornaments but rather what God chooses to give and distribute there.

After everyone found their places in the pew, Jerry put his head down in prayer. Ben and Jessica also noticed that Helen was showing Olivia a prayer on the inside cover of the hymnal. Apparently, it was a prayer that was prayed individually by the church members before the worship service began. Olivia folded her hands with Helen, and they both quietly prayed the prayer together. After Jerry finished praying, he looked over at the Campbells for a moment before quietly getting up, walking to the back of the church, and returning with several bulletins, which he handed to Ben and Jessica.

REVERENCE

The most proper response to the realm of the sacred within the sanctuary is reverence. But what does it look like to be reverent? Reverence is not necessarily sad or serious. Reverence is not being irritated or fearful. Reverence is not being super religious or overtly pious. Reverence is not a disposition of cranky parishioners who are angry at the world or a prudish group of people reacting to the excesses of the world.

Instead, reverence means acting with humility. See Matthew 8:2; 9:18; 14:33; 15:25, where a word translated as "worship" or "knelt down" is used to communicate reverence, awe, and homage before the sacred Christ.

Soon a man in his sixties walked slowly from the back of the church to the altar at the front. He bowed at the altar, turned to the congregation, and said, "Please rise and turn to page fifteen."

Noah had already grabbed a hymnal for himself, and since Helen and Olivia were sharing another, only one hymnal was left in front of Ben and Jessica. Ben reached for it and opened it to page 15, holding it out for Jessica to share with him. Jessica put a hand on her side of the hymnal, and they smiled at each other briefly as they enjoyed the moment of togetherness.

The pastor looked up at the small congregation of about sixty people and said, "In the name of the Father and of the Son and of the Holy Spirit." After a brief pause, he continued, "Let us confess our sins to God our Father."

CONFESSION

After King David committed adultery with Bathsheba and had her husband murdered, he confessed his sins and said, "You [Lord] forgave the iniquity of my sin" (Psalm 32:5). Thus, the church confesses King David's words boldly because we know that just as the Lord forgave David, so He is faithful and just to forgive us. The church confesses David's words because we stand with King David as sinners in need of forgiveness. (See also 2 Samuel 11.)

The members of Immanuel Church then bowed their heads in silence. Even though the silence lasted only about ten seconds, it was extremely sobering and different from what the Campbells had experienced elsewhere. Instead of talking about the church's ministries, the activities of the week, politics, mercy care, or the denomination, Immanuel Church was silent.

The pastor broke the silence, and the church began speaking together, "O almighty God, merciful Father, I, a poor, miserable sinner, confess unto You all my sin and iniquities . . ."

As they spoke the words of confession together, Ben and Jessica shared a look. Even without saying anything, they knew the other was thinking about their unresolved fight from Friday night. Ben nodded as if to say, "I messed up." Jessica nodded back as if to say, "Me too."

After the confession of sin, the pastor walked up several steps, placed his hand on the baptismal font, and turned to face the church. With a serious but joyful disposition, he loudly proclaimed, "Upon this your confession, I, by the virtue of my office as a called servant of Jesus, announce the grace of God unto you all. In the place and by the command of Jesus, I forgive you all your sins."

Ben had a million thoughts rushing through his head at this point. For starters, he found it refreshing to see the pastor standing at the front, confessing his sins along with the rest of the congregation—as if he were a sinner leading other sinners. Ben had also appreciated hearing the words of forgiveness the pastor had spoken, but he wondered, Did the pastor really have that power? And why had he made a point to place his hand on the place where babies were baptized?

ABSOLUTION

Jesus breathed on His disciples and gave His Spirit to them because He was sending them into the world to deliver the forgiveness of sins that He had won by His death and resurrection. (See John 20:19–31.) And so, the Words of Absolution spoken by the pastor during worship are Jesus' words of forgiveness, not the words of a man in a white robe. That man is only a poor, miserable sinner, just like his flock. (See Matthew 18:18.) Rather, Jesus makes use of a man's mouth to breathe life into His people, to chase away death and fill them with His life and His forgiveness.

The congregation continued by singing a simple song that everyone seemed to know. The words were a humble plea for mercy, even though the tune didn't sound sad.

After the song for mercy, the congregation sang a song of praise. This song, like the previous one, was obviously familiar to the church, but it was different from any singing the Campbells had done before. Certain notes were held for a long time, which gave the song an older feel.

THE KYRIE: A CRY FOR MERCY

Bartimaeus was a blind beggar. He cried out to Christ for mercy. His cry for mercy was a cry of faith to receive pity and compassion from Christ. The church sings Bartimaeus's words because we, too, need the Lord's compassion. (See Mark 10:46–52.)

The service continued with prayer and Scripture readings, which were printed in the plain, black-and-white bulletins that Jerry had handed them. Ben, with his type-A personality, could not help but notice that the folding crease was uneven and that there were several typos, including several wrong dates on the events listed for the week. Then they turned back to the hymnals to confess the Nicene Creed and sing a hymn.

THE IMPORTANCE OF CREEDS

Creeds are confessions of faith. The Apostles' Creed and the Nicene Creed, the two most common Christian creeds, help teach Christians and guard the church against errors. Furthermore, creeds help keep the church focused on the main thing: God's creative, redemptive, and sanctifying work. We can confess the creeds loudly and confidently, for they summarize what God the Father has done for His people through the life, death, and resurrection of His Son, Jesus Christ.

As they sang, Jessica looked at the bottom of the page. Printed in small font was the name of the hymn's author and when it was written. Taken aback, Jessica pointed at it so that Ben would see it: "Text: Thomas à Kempis, 1380–1471; Tune: English, 15th century." It was hard to believe they were singing a song that was six hundred years old. Still, they didn't have trouble singing along with the simple melody, except that the organist seemed to pause every two measures. Looking over to the right of the altar area, Jessica noticed that the organist would pause, look up at the music, and then look down at the organ keys to play. Then she would pause, look up at the music again, and then look down at the organ keys to play. The pauses weren't overly distracting, but it was obvious that the organist was by no means a professional.

HYMNS STAND THE TEST OF TIME

An old hymn from 1450 is more popular than a song on top of the Billboard Hot 100. Wait, really? Think of it this way. The majority of popular songs from this past year will not be remembered in five years. After fifty years, only a handful of songs will be remembered. What about five hundred years from now? Even fewer will have stood the test of time. And so, a hymn from the fifteenth century being sung in thousands of churches around the world for the last five hundred years is truly more popular than one of the top songs on the Billboard Hot 100.

During the last stanza, Ben noticed the pastor get up and walk to the altar area, kneeling at the rail in front of it. He bowed his head and was obviously praying. As the hymn came to a close, the pastor slowly rose, using the rail to push himself up. He walked to the pulpit, raised his hand, and made the sign of the cross while saying, "In the name of Jesus. Amen."

PRIMARILY ABOUT THE EAR

God put ears on sinners so that they would listen to His Word. (See Romans 10:17.) This means that Christians are best represented by the human ear, not the human hand or mouth. As an ear, you are not meant to primarily give and do things for Christ but primarily to receive all good things from Christ. (See also Matthew 13:9.)

The pastor delivered the sermon using handwritten notes, and he looked down at them often. The lack of eye contact did not seem to matter to the members of Immanuel Church, as it was apparent that everyone was listening. The sermon did not have many cultural references or personal stories. Instead, the pastor spoke very directly of what God expected of the members of Immanuel. Referring to the Old Testament Reading, which was read earlier, he described how Christians often create idols in their lives by fearing, loving, and trusting things other than God Almighty. He then referenced the reading from Ephesians and commented about factions in the church over an apparent struggle over cemetery plots. Even though the pastor did not raise his voice, his words fell like a hammer. He was not holding back from being truthful to the church.

Jessica found herself being a bit worried, as it seemed like he was calling out current struggles between the members of the church. Yet as she looked around, the members of the church seemed to be okay with the confrontational sermon, as if they expected to be confronted about their sins.

After several more minutes of preaching, the pastor paused. Then he said, "Baptized saints of Immanuel, the Lord calls you to repent of your idols, to repent of your backbiting, and to repent of your factions."

He paused again, collected his thoughts, and then looked out and said clearly, "You are to repent and hear the Gospel that the Lord has called you all out of darkness, placed you in His light, kept you in the ark of His church, and wrapped a robe of righteousness around you, covering all your sins. Do not forget who you are! You do not belong to gossip, slander, or vain idols! You belong to Christ, and Christ belongs to you."

Glancing down at his manuscript again, Pastor Reynolds continued with even more conviction in his voice, "Perhaps we could summarize all of this by saying that here at Immanuel Church, we are in this together under the grace of God. Each of us, as Christians, endures the same hard world, with the same foul devil, with the same stubborn sinful nature. Yet, equally, we have been forgiven, redeemed, and claimed by God through Christ. And so, today and in the weeks to come, we walk in Jesus—always being for one another—no matter the sin and no matter the conflict. Since we are in this together, we seek restoration and forgiveness at every opportunity. Indeed, because of Jesus, we share one another's burdens. We are quick to confess and quick to forgive. Baptized saints, because there is more grace in Jesus than there is sin in us, we will not grow weary in doing good and extending grace and forgiveness to one another."

The sermon ended then, and the pastor led the church in the Lord's Prayer before moving in front of the altar and singing some words about Communion. He wasn't the best singer, Ben thought, but then again, he wasn't really singing. He was speaking a Bible verse while letting a tune come through at the same time. It kind of sounded like the tune was wrapping itself around the words.

An usher then began directing members up toward the altar. Ben leaned over and said, "This must be Communion. Do we go up there?"

Whispering back, Jessica said, "Yes, Jerry told me before that we should come up to receive a blessing. I can tell you more after the service. He said that if we ever want to join the church, then we would take Communion after becoming members."

The usher came to the pew where the Campbells were sitting. They stood and walked to the altar up front, moving slowly at Helen's pace. Even though their old church in Fairview had Communion once every three months, this seemed different and more important.

As they all gathered in front of the rail, the pastor said, "Welcome to the Lord's Table."

Jerry and Helen bowed slightly and knelt, so the Campbells did the same, following their lead. Even though Jerry was a former Vietnam vet who carried himself with warm confidence, his disposition at the rail was like a beggar. Though Ben was not trying to peek, he saw Jerry hit his chest with his fist while whispering, "God, be merciful to me, the sinner."

The pastor came toward Jerry, held up some bread and a silver cup with wine, and said, "Jerry, the body and blood of Christ—for you."

Jerry received the bread and wine and then exhaled, his body relaxing and his face filling with gratitude, before whispering, "Thank You, Jesus."

COMMUNION: A MEAL FOR SINNERS

The holy meal of Communion is for the forgiveness of sins, which means that it is for sinners. (See Matthew 26:28.) And so, those who see themselves as sin-sick people find great comfort at the Lord's Table. Indeed, the church is a hospital for sinners, not a country club for the self-righteous and the self-sufficient. To the point, to be worthy of the Lord's body and blood is to realize that one is unworthy, yet at the same time believe upon Jesus' words, "Given and shed for you for the forgiveness of sins." What a gift to know that the Lord Jesus truly gives Himself in, with, and under the elements for the forgiveness of sins and the strengthening of the faith. (See 1 Corinthians 11:27–29.)

The pastor dismissed them, and they returned to their pew. Ben gazed at the crucifix up front, sitting quietly as the rest of the congregation took their turn at the altar. He realized that none of the other churches they had visited over the past three months had had a cross this prominent with a crucified and bloodied Jesus.

This got him thinking even more. What made Immanuel Church so different? It did not have a better customer experience than The Quest. There was no large fellowship hall or busy weekly schedule like Parkside Community Fellowship. Unlike Mercy Hill, there were no backpacks or soup kitchen. Did the pews of Immanuel hold people of importance? Perhaps, but if so, they did not make themselves noticeable like at First Church of Midway. The sermon did not focus on ways to improve yourself, like Pastor Jonathan and Cornerstone. And so far out in the country, Immanuel certainly didn't have any big politicians or movers and shakers in the community like Peace Bible Church.

And while Immanuel Church certainly seemed to belong to a denomination, it was not on prominent display like at Trinity.

So what did Immanuel Church have? In the eyes of the world, nothing except for bitter coffee, a bulletin full of typos, and an organist who could not hold a consistent beat.

HE CHOOSES THE WEAK, ORDINARY, AND FOOLISH

God chooses what the world considers nonsense, weak, and ordinary not only to shame but also to destroy all pretentious thinking and inflated pride. Remember that God chose a slave nation called Israel to bring forth the Messiah, not mighty Egypt, Assyria, or Babylon. He chose a stinky manger and a bloody cross to accomplish salvation, not a golden throne and a mighty sword. Also, who can forget that a bunch of fishermen and a tax collector were chosen to equip the early church? The Lord continues to choose His own not because of their skill, power, influence, wisdom, or nobility. He does not even choose because of ethnicity, status, or gender. He certainly does not choose because of religious heritage. No, you are chosen by Christ and for Christ so that He can spiritually clothe you of your nakedness, feed you in your hunger, and wash away your grime as a sheer gift. He does this so that the only thing that you can boast about is Christ. (See 1 Corinthians 1:17–31.)

Ben wrestled with these thoughts a bit more, his head lowered in contemplation. What kept him and his family from returning to the previous churches? Why was his family left feeling incomplete, even though all the previous churches had so many great things going for them? Why did he find himself willing to consider such a long drive to church each Sunday to go to Immanuel Church when it had nothing enticing compared to the other churches around Midway? What were those other churches missing? What did Immanuel have?

Movement at the front of the church brought Ben out of his thoughts a bit. The pastor had returned to the altar area after serving Communion to some people in the pews who couldn't come up to the front.

The pastor announced, "The true body and blood of our Lord Jesus Christ strengthen you and preserve you in body and soul to life everlasting. Go in peace; your sins are forgiven in Jesus."

That's it! Ben realized. What were the other churches missing or, at best, forgetting? What did Immanuel have and emphasize?

Jesus.

Ben looked over at Jessica and their kids and felt a burden lifted off his shoulders. This church's purpose and unity were clear and simple: Jesus alone. Immanuel Church was the home that the Campbells always had but recently discovered!

Jessica caught Ben's eye and smiled. She leaned in and whispered, "I think we've been given a church home."

Chapter 8 Study Guide

REVIEW

1. What unites the members of Immanuel Church?
2. What is the purpose of Immanuel Church?
3. How did the architecture, floor plans, furnishings, sights, and sounds convey the unity and purpose of Immanuel Church?

DISCUSS

1. Compare the message preached at Immanuel with the messages mentioned at the other churches. What is the problem mentioned, and what is the solution offered for each?
2. Can the message preached at Immanuel still be found in a nicer building that offers better coffee? If so, could the message preached at Immanuel be preached at the other churches around Midway? Why or why not? How do you think each congregation would respond if the Immanuel sermon was read in their respective churches?
3. What is the significance of having a graveyard around a church? Did you find it peculiar that one of the tombstones said "Lazarus, come out"?
4. How does the church prepare us for death?

REFLECT

1. What did Immanuel Church have that the other churches did not?

Will the Real Church Please Stand Up?

As we learned along with the Campbell family, the real church is not defined by great customer service, social bonds, humanitarian efforts, cultural influence, personal improvements, political impact, or denominational commitment. Rather, most of these would be considered peripheral indicators of the church. In other words, one may find the church among such things as church polity, traditions, and rituals, but it is not guaranteed. Instead, the true church is found where believers gather around Christ's Word and Sacraments. (See the Augsburg Confession, Article V.)

This means that no matter how beautiful the architecture of a church may be, no matter how pious the parishioners may seem, no matter how many good works a church may do, no matter how busy or large a church may be, and no matter how organized the polity is, if there is no Word of God and Sacraments, there is no church at all. In fact, there is sadly a false church in its place. Whenever a church unites around something other than Christ, whenever a church's fundamental purpose is something other than to proclaim the forgiveness of sins to sinners, then it is no church at all. The real church is found where the people's unity is Christ and their purpose is to proclaim Him crucified and raised for us. Thus, a tiny church with ten members that rests in God's Word is ten times larger than a church of a thousand that does not teach the Word of God. For Christ is the Word of God, and He is what we poor, miserable sinners need more than anything else in this world. This is what humanity has been missing since the fall into sin and what we will continue to need until the end of the age.

And so, what is missing at Immanuel Church? One could argue good coffee, but more important is this: it lacks the man-centered theology that all the other churches had. Instead, Christ is properly on the throne of power and proclaimed as the center, purpose, and unity of the church.

The members of the real church gather around Christ and His gifts. Recall how the pastor at Immanuel placed his hand on the baptismal font to pronounce forgiveness. Recall the simple and direct proclamation of the Word. Remember how they confessed the same faith with one another and the millions who came before them through the Creed. Recall the centrality of the Lord's Supper and how everyone knelt together. The members of Immanuel Church knew they were missing everything and that nothing except Jesus Christ and Him crucified could fill their need of a Savior from sin.

What was the purpose of Immanuel Church? Olive Benson's tombstone outside the church inscribed with the words "Lazarus, come out!" gives us a hint. The purpose of the true church is for believers to be kept safe in the holy ark of the church until death, and thus we are brought at last to our heavenly home to see Jesus face to face in the joys of paradise along with those who have departed in the faith. At Immanuel Church, the pastor shepherds parishioners from the baptismal font to the communion rail to their holy graves. And so, the purpose of the real church is for its people to abide in Christ until their bodily resurrection on the Last Day.

We Christians are prone to wander. We are prone to leave God, who loves us. We are like sheep who wander to other pastures. We are like coins that seem to get lost in deep cracks. We are like unruly children who go to the big city to party. (See Luke 15.) Our sinful nature loves to lead us away from Jesus. (See Romans 7:15.) But that is not how the Christian faith works. Indeed, we Christians cannot live independently from Christ and His gifts. Just as we need air to breathe, water to live, and food to give us energy, we need Christ for the forgiveness, life, and salvation that we are missing and can't provide for ourselves. (See John 15:3–5.)

Thus, our Christian life is circular because we must keep returning from our wanderings to the fountainhead of grace and truth. We return not just at the beginning or end of life but constantly throughout our lives and days. In other words, we abide in Jesus. With reverence, we return to Him like little children to receive our full royal inheritance. (See Matthew 18:1–4.) And the Lord? He does not despise our return to Him. We are not a nuisance. We are not a bother. He longs to hear our confession. (See Psalm 51:17.) He has joy in giving us forgiveness in His gifts. He desires to give Himself to us and to bless us, not just at the beginning or the end of our lives but constantly as we abide in Him. And so we come each week to church, gathering with other believers to receive His gifts, even as we daily repent of our sins and return to the reality of our Baptism.

The tower of Babel—that great and impressive work of mankind—crumbled long ago. However, it is constantly being built in each of our hearts as we seek to make a name for ourselves, to impress others and God as we perpetually try to climb higher and higher. Churches that help us build these towers will not stand. They are not a sure foundation but sinking sands offering false hope and ladders to nowhere. These churches are false because they unite us around ourselves instead of preaching and delivering the Word, Christ Jesus.

There is only one true tower, Christ Jesus. All other walls will crumble to the ground as the kingdom of heaven continues to shine forth, high and lifted up, with Christ's nail-pierced hands extending into the rubble of mankind's failed projects and displaced unity. The real church stands in Christ alone. Where Jesus is, there you will find the real church standing.

Leader Guide

Chapter 1: The Quest

REVIEW

1. What unites the members of The Quest?
   - *The members are united by a good customer experience.*

2. What is the purpose of The Quest?
   - *The end purpose is an undefined journey.*

3. How did the architecture, floor plans, furnishings, sights, and sounds convey the unity and purpose of The Quest?
   - *Take special note of the first-time parking, the parking attendant, the electric padded seats, the premium coffee, the separation of the children from the parents, and so on. These all aid in advancing a good customer experience.*

DISCUSS

1. Why is it important to know the end goal—the purpose—of the church?
   - *Please consult the text box titled "Telos" (p. 14) and 1 Corinthians 15:3–4.*

2. How does the center of the church influence the services, members, and church leadership?
   - *Please consult the text box titled "Koinonia" (pp. 19–20) and 1 Corinthians 1:9.*

3. Why do you think the children were separated from Ben and Jessica? Should children be separated from their parents in church? Does this strengthen or weaken the family?
   - *Please consult the text box titled "Divided-Family versus Family-Integrated Churches" (p. 10) as well as Malachi 4:4–6 and Psalm 78:5–8.*

4. Why does a church like The Quest need to base a sermon on a movie? What are the dangers of doing this?
   - *Please consult the text box titled "Into the Bible or out of the Bible?" (p. 16) and 2 Timothy 4:1–5.*

REFLECT

1. Jessica said that something was missing from The Quest. What is missing?
   - *By the end of this book, the answer to this question will become clear, but encourage the group to discuss what might be missing based on their own interactions and impressions of this chapter. Your group may want to contemplate 1 Corinthians 15:3–8 as part of this discussion.*

Chapter 2: Parkside Community Fellowship Church

REVIEW

1. What unites the members of Parkside Community Fellowship Church?
   - *The members are united by friendship.*

2. What is the purpose of Parkside Community Fellowship Church?
   - *Its end purpose is to be sectarian.*

3. How did the architecture, floor plans, furnishings, sights, and sounds convey the unity and purpose of Parkside Community Fellowship Church?
   - *Take special note that the main entrance to the church was the gym. Also, take note of the amount of time members spent in the fireside room. The upkeep of the sanctuary should also be noted compared to the rest of the facility.*

DISCUSS

1. Have you ever thought about how church architecture and building layout can communicate the purpose of a local church?
   - *Please consult the text boxes titled "Church Building Layout" (p. 27) and "Sanctuary Architecture" (pp. 30–31).*

2. What does a monastic approach offer churchgoers?

   - *Please consult the text boxes titled "Church Schedules and Monasteries" (pp. 32–33) and "Sectarianism" (p. 34) as well as the content on page 36.*

3. Why could a focus on friendship prove detrimental to a church's foundation?

   - *Please consult the content on page 37.*

4. The chapter stated, "Churches are not meant to be monasteries, and the health of the local church should not necessarily be tied to the religious fervor or bustle inside the walls of the church." Do you agree or disagree?

   - *Please consult the content on page 36.*

REFLECT

1. Ben said that something seemed to be missing from Parkside. What is missing?

   - *By the end of this book, the answer to this question will become clear, but encourage the group to discuss what might be missing based on their own interactions and impressions of this chapter. Your group may want to contemplate 1 Corinthians 15:3–8 as part of this discussion.*

Chapter 3: Mercy Hill Church

REVIEW

1. What unites the members of Mercy Hill Church?
   - *The members are united by filling the void of the broken family.*

2. What is the purpose of Mercy Hill Church?
   - *Its end purpose is to provide mercy care.*

3. How did the architecture, floor plans, furnishings, sights, and sounds convey the unity and purpose of Mercy Hill Church?
   - *Take special note of the message on the banners, the attached soup kitchen, and the backpacks in the entrance area of the church. These all show the focus of mercy care.*

DISCUSS

1. If you had to write a mission statement for Mercy Hill Church, what would it say?
   - *It is helpful to keep in mind that Mercy Hill Church is attempting to stand in the gap of broken families. Consider Bill's deep sentiments in this chapter to help answer this question (see pp. 48–49).*

2. Do you agree with Mercy Hill Church's pastor that we should preach the Gospel at all times and, if necessary, use words?
   - *Please consult the text box titled "Great Commission versus Great Commandment" (pp. 44–45).*

3. How would you describe the difference between the Great Commandment and the Great Commission?
   - *Please consult the text box titled "Great Commission versus Great Commandment" (pp. 44–45). Especially compare Matthew 28:18–20 and 22:36–40.*

4. How would you describe the three estates to a member at Mercy Hill Church?
   - *Please consult the text box titled "The Three Estates" (pp. 47–48), the book of Titus, and the Table of Duties in Luther's Small Catechism.*

REFLECT

1. Jessica told Olivia, "The church is not just a food pantry or soup kitchen. There must be something more." What more is needed at Mercy Hill Church?
   - *By the end of this book, the answer to this question will become clear, but encourage the group to discuss what might be missing based on their own interactions and impressions of this chapter. Your group may want to contemplate 1 Corinthians 15:3–8 as part of this discussion.*

Chapter 4: First Church of Midway

REVIEW

1. What unites the members of First Church of Midway?
   - *The members are united by social validation.*

2. What is the purpose of First Church of Midway?
   - *Its end purpose is to be noticed.*

3. How did the architecture, floor plans, furnishings, sights, and sounds convey the unity and purpose of First Church of Midway?
   - *Take special note of the giving wall, stamped name inside the hymnal, and location of the church next to the mayor's mansion and district court building. Notice how Jess and Ben were excluded from the conversation when the mayor arrived.*

DISCUSS

1. Think of a time when you did not feel accepted. What was it about the social setting that caused you to notice you did not fit in?
   - *Let participants discuss their experiences. As necessary, consult the text box titled "King of the Hill" (p. 59). See also the biblical references in this text box: Philippians 3:4–11; Luke 11:43; 14:7–11.*

2. Does the biblical church take a person's worldly status or abilities into consideration when it comes to the doctrine of justification?
   - *Please consult the text box titled "Kingdom of Heaven" (pp. 65–66) and especially Galatians 3:28.*

3. **If good works are good, why is it problematic in the church to do them for all to see?**
   - *Please consult the text box titled "The World as a Stage" (pp. 64–65) as well as Matthew 6:1–4 and 1 Corinthians 1:27.*

4. **Why was it not important for the mayor to be at church consistently?**
   - *Please consult the content on page 64.*

REFLECT

1. **Noah said, "It felt like something was missing at that church today. I don't want to go back." What was missing from First Church of Midway?**
   - *By the end of this book, the answer to this question will become clear, but encourage the group to discuss what might be missing based on their own interactions and impressions of this chapter. Your group may want to contemplate 1 Corinthians 15:3–8 as part of this discussion.*

Chapter 5: Cornerstone Community Church

REVIEW

1. What unites the members of Cornerstone Community Church?
   - *The members are united by moralistic intragroup competition.*

2. What is the purpose of Cornerstone Community Church?
   - *Its end purpose is to arrive at a self-improved utopic bliss.*

3. How did the architecture, floor plans, furnishings, sights, and sounds convey the unity and purpose of Cornerstone Community Church?
   - *Take special note of the Resource Center, the theme of the sermon, and the titles of the books. Notice the similar themes of the books and their content.*

DISCUSS

1. Can mankind ever arrive at a perfect political, economic, and social utopia? Why or why not?
   - *Please consult the text box titled "Chasing Eden" (p. 75).*

2. Pastor Jonathan shared five practical tips in his sermon. Where did this pastor point his congregation for answers?
   - *Please consult the text box titled "Inward versus Outward" (pp. 79–80) and Jeremiah 17:9. Notice that Jeremiah lists our heart as the problem, not the solution. Also consider the Bible passages in the text box; the biblical authors point us not inward to ourselves but outward to Christ!*

3. How can pastors become spiritual manipulators with the kind of theology present at Cornerstone Community Church?

   - Please consult pages 77–78.

4. Why did Ben become agitated by the man who invited them to be a part of the church activities?

   - Please consult pages 77–78. This question ties in to the answers to the question above.

REFLECT

1. Do you agree with Jessica's final observations about Cornerstone's purpose?

   - Encourage the group to discuss whether they agree or disagree with Jessica's observations and what might be missing from Cornerstone. Your group may want to contemplate 1 Corinthians 15:3–8 as part of this discussion.

Chapter 6: Peace Bible Church

REVIEW

1. What unites the members of Peace Bible Church?
   - *The members are united by a common political association.*

2. What is the purpose of Peace Bible Church?
   - *Its end purpose is to advance political policy.*

3. How did the architecture, floor plans, furnishings, sights, and sounds convey the unity and purpose of Peace Bible Church?
   - *Take special note of the marketing of the annual Faith Emancipation Conference, the large American flag in the sanctuary, the message on the sign, and the political insert in the bulletin.*

DISCUSS

1. How would you respond if your pastor announced a political sentiment with which you adamantly disagreed?
   - *Please consult the text box titled "What Not to Expect in a Sermon" (pp. 89–90).*

2. Is it fair to say that just as Mercy Hill Church overstepped into the estate of the family, Peace Bible Church is overstepping into the estate of the government?
   - *Please consult the text box titled "Give unto Caesar and unto God" (p. 91) and Matthew 22:21.*

WILL THE REAL CHURCH PLEASE STAND UP?

3. Is there a time and place when a church and Christians
   should disobey and speak against the government?
   - *Please consult the text box titled "Disobeying, Bearing
   Witness, and Changing Policy" (p. 93).*

4. What is the difference between a Christian judge and
   a judge who is Christian? Why is this subtle distinction important to understand?
   - *Please consult the text box titled "How Churches
   Influence Politics" (p. 94).*

REFLECT

1. Ben said, "It seems that a church should balance the
   important issues while also not neglecting what the church
   is supposed to be about." What should Peace Bible Church
   be about?
   - *By the end of this book, the answer to this question will
   become clear, but encourage the group to discuss what
   might be missing based on their own interactions and
   impressions of this chapter. Your group may want to contemplate 1 Corinthians 15:3–8 as part of this discussion.*

Chapter 7: Trinity Church

REVIEW

1. What unites the members of Trinity Church?
   - *The members are united by denominational heritage.*

2. What is the purpose of Trinity Church?
   - *Its end purpose is denominational allegiance.*

3. How did the architecture, floor plans, furnishings, sights, and sounds convey the unity and purpose of Trinity Church?
   - *Take special note of the use of the denominational logo on its signage, pins, and bulletins. The hallway of presidents also shows denominational loyalty. Finally, the reference to the denominational programs in the conversations conveys its unity and purpose.*

DISCUSS

1. How are denominations beneficial for members and for those trying to find a church home?
   - *Please consult the text box titled "What Is a Denomination?" (p. 100).*

2. Some churches avoid denominations and call themselves nondenominational. Why do you think they want that distinctive label?
   - *Please consult the text box titled "Authoritative Sources for Theology" (p. 106).*

3. What did Noah offer as a suggestion to his parents for how to belong to the new church? Do you think if the Campbells had been related, it would have changed how they felt about Trinity Church?
   - *Please consult the text box titled "Denominational Nepotism" (p. 102).*

4. This chapter briefly mentioned that the sermon of the day was about loyalty. To whom do we owe our loyalty as Christians?
   - *Please consult the text box titled "Heritage, Traditions, and Policies" (p. 107).*

REFLECT

1. Jessica said, "I think something is still missing if we feel like we need to do ancestry research or run for a position to belong." What was missing from Trinity Church?
   - *By the end of this book, the answer to this question will become clear, but encourage the group to discuss what might be missing based on their own interactions and impressions of this chapter. Your group may want to contemplate 1 Corinthians 15:3–8 as part of this discussion.*

Chapter 8: Immanuel Church

REVIEW

1. What unites the members of Immanuel Church?
   - *The members are united by Christ and His gifts.*

2. What is the purpose of Immanuel Church?
   - *Its end purpose is to abide in Christ unto death.*

3. How did the architecture, floor plans, furnishings, sights, and sounds convey the unity and purpose of Immanuel Church?
   - *Take special note of the graveyard, crucifix, use of the hymnals, and focus of the service leading to communion. They all lead to the Word and Sacraments.*

DISCUSS

1. Compare the message preached at Immanuel with the messages mentioned at the other churches. What is the problem mentioned, and what is the solution offered for each?
   - *Take special note of what the pastor confronted in the sermon—the idols of the heart (see p. 125).*

2. Can the message preached at Immanuel still be found in a nicer building that offers better coffee? If so, could the message preached at Immanuel be preached at the other churches around Midway? Why or why not? How do you think each congregation would respond if the Immanuel sermon was read in their respective churches?
   - *Please consult the text box titled "Doctrine and Practice" (pp. 4–5) from the introduction to this book.*

If Immanuel's sermon had been preached in one of the other churches, the doctrine in the sermon would collide with the various practices of that church. In other words, the church's architecture, furnishings, sights, and sounds would be conveying a different purpose and unity than what the sermon preached.

3. What is the significance of having a graveyard around a church? Did you find it peculiar that one of the tombstones said "Lazarus, come out"?

   - Please consult the text box titled "Lazarus, Come Out!" (pp. 116–17).

4. How does the church prepare us for death?

   - Let participants discuss. As necessary, direct them to the conclusion of the book, particularly the comments there explaining Olive Benson's tombstone (see p. 134).

REFLECT

1. What did Immanuel Church have that the other churches did not?

   - Read 1 Corinthians 15:3–8. Consider how Paul says that the Gospel is the beginning, middle, and end of our salvation. Paul does not appeal to anything except the weightiest article of faith—the Gospel! The Lutheran Confessions repeat this, saying, "The first and chief article is this: Jesus Christ, our God and Lord, died for our sins and was raised again for our justification (Romans 4:24–25). He alone is the Lamb of God who takes away the sins of the world (John 1:29), and God has laid upon Him the iniquities of us all (Isaiah 53:6)" (Smalcald Articles, Part II, Article I, paragraphs 1–3).

The message of the Gospel for the forgiveness of sins must always be kept pure and front and center. It must be returned to again and again, "for it is the power of God for salvation" (Romans 1:16).

Church Chart

CHURCH	UNITY	PURPOSE
THE QUEST	GOOD CUSTOMER EXPERIENCE	JOURNEY WITH NO DESTINATION
PARKSIDE COMMUNITY FELLOWSHIP CHURCH	FRIENDSHIP	BEING SECTARIAN
MERCY HILL CHURCH	FILLING THE VOID OF BROKEN FAMILIES	PROVIDING MERCY CARE
FIRST CHURCH OF MIDWAY	SOCIAL VALIDATION	BEING NOTICED
CORNERSTONE COMMUNITY CHURCH	MORALISTIC INTRAGROUP COMPETITION	ARRIVING AT A SELF-IMPROVED UTOPIC BLISS
PEACE BIBLE CHURCH	COMMON POLITICAL ASSOCIATION	ADVANCING POLITICAL POLICY
TRINITY CHURCH	DENOMINATIONAL HERITAGE	DENOMINATIONAL ALLEGIANCE
IMMANUEL CHURCH	CHRIST AND HIS GIFTS	ABIDING IN CHRIST UNTO DEATH

Text Box Index